LANDMARKS OF
THE AMERICAN REVOLUTION

In CONGRESS, July 4, 1776.

The unanimous Declaration of the thirteen united States of America,

American Landmarks

JAMES OLIVER HORTON
General Editor

LANDMARKS OF

THE AMERICAN REVOLUTION

Gary B. Nash

OXFORD
UNIVERSITY PRESS

Published in association with the
National Register of Historic Places, National Park Service, the National Parks Foundation
and the Gilder Lehrman Institute of American History

OXFORD
UNIVERSITY PRESS

Oxford   New York
Auckland   Bangkok   Buenos Aires   Cape Town   Chennai
Dar es Salaam   Delhi   Hong Kong   Istanbul   Karachi   Kolkata
Kuala Lumpur   Madrid   Melbourne   Mexico City   Mumbai   Nairobi
São Paulo   Shanghai   Singapore   Taipei   Tokyo   Toronto

Published by Oxford University Press, Inc.
198 Madison Avenue, New York, New York 10016
www.oup.com

Oxford is a registered trademark of Oxford University Press

Library of Congress Cataloging-in-Publication Data

Nash, Gary B.
  Landmarks of the American Revolution / Gary B. Nash.
      p. cm. — (American landmarks)
"Published in association with the National Register of Historic Places,
National Park Service, and the National Parks Foundation."
Includes bibliographical references and index.
  ISBN 0-19-512849-4 (alk. paper)
1. Historic sites—United States. 2. United States—History—Revolution,
1775–1783—Battlefields. 3. United States—History—Revolution,
1775–1783—Monuments. 4. United States—History, Local. I. Title.
II. American landmarks (Oxford University Press)
  E159 .N26 2003
  973.3—dc21   2002014152

Printing number: 9 8 7 6 5 4 3 2 1

Printed in Hong Kong
on acid-free paper

Cover: *Philadelphia's Independence Hall, known as the Pennsylvania State House during the American Revolution, was the site of the signing of the Declaration of Independence.*

Frontispiece: *The Declaration of Independence puts into words the principles the patriots fought for during the American Revolution.*

Title page: *On December 16, 1773, the Sons of Liberty, some dressed as Indians, dumped tea into Boston Harbor to protest the British tax policies.*

American Landmarks

JAMES OLIVER HORTON
General Editor

Landmarks of African-American History

Landmarks of American Immigration

Landmarks of American Indian History

Landmarks of American Literature

Landmarks of the American Presidents

Landmarks of American Religion

Landmarks of the American Revolution

Landmarks of American Science & Invention

Landmarks of American Sports

Landmarks of American Women's History

Landmarks of the Civil War

Landmarks of Liberty

Landmarks of the Old South

LANDMARKS OF
The American Revolution

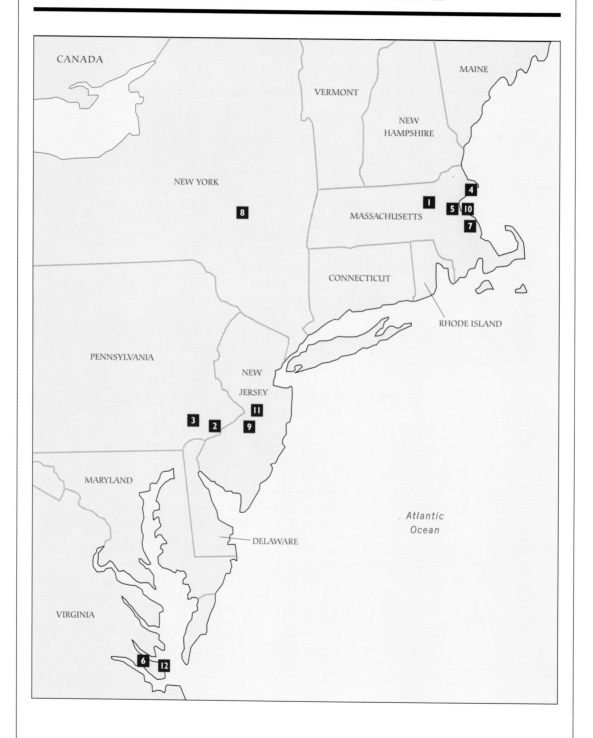

CANADA

MAINE

VERMONT

NEW
HAMPSHIRE

NEW YORK

8

MASSACHUSETTS

1 **4**

5 **10**

7

CONNECTICUT

RHODE ISLAND

PENNSYLVANIA

NEW
JERSEY

11

3 **2** **9**

MARYLAND

DELAWARE

*Atlantic
Ocean*

VIRGINIA

6 **12**

Contents

PAGE 14
Lexington Green

PAGE 86
Johnson Hall

PAGE 108
Old South Meeting House

Introduction:
The Power of Place

James Oliver Horton

General Editor

Few experiences can connect us with our past more completely than walking the ground where our history happened. The landmarks of American history have a vital role to play in helping us to understand our past, because they are its physical evidence. The sensory experience of a place can help us to reconstruct historical events, just as archaeologists reconstruct vanished civilizations. It can also inspire us to empathy with those who came before us. A place can take hold of us, body, mind, and spirit. As philosophers of the Crow Indian nation have reminded us, "The ground on which we stand is sacred ground. It is the blood of our ancestors." It is the history owed to our children. They will remember that history only to the extent that we preserve the places where it was made.

Historical sites are some of history's best teachers. In the early 1970s, when I was a graduate student in Boston, working on a study of the nineteenth-century black community of that city, I walked the streets of Beacon Hill imagining the daily lives of those who lived there a century before. Although I had learned much about the people of that community from their newspapers and pamphlets, from their personal letters and official records, nothing put me in touch with their lives and their time like standing in the places where they had stood and exploring the neighborhood where they lived.

I remember walking along Myrtle Street just down Beacon Hill from the rear of the Massachusetts State House in the early morning and realizing that Leonard Grimes, the black minister of the Fugitive Slave Church, must have squinted into the sun just as I was doing as he emerged from his home at the rear of number 59 and turned left on his way to his church. Walking up Joy Street in December added new meaning to descriptions I had read about the sound of children sledding down its slope during the particularly snowy winter of 1850. And twisting my ankle on irregular cobblestone streets made clear the precarious footing for fugitive slaves fleeing at full run from slave catchers empowered by the Fugitive Slave Law of 1850.

Any historical event is much better understood within the context of its historical setting. It is one thing to read the details of the Battle of Gettysburg. It is quite another to stand on Little Round Top, with its commanding view of the battlefield to the north and west, and contemplate the assault of the Fifteenth Alabama Confederates against the downhill charge of the Twentieth Maine Volunteer Infantry. Standing at the summit, taking the measure of the degree of slope and the open area that afforded little cover to advancing armies is an unforgettable experience. It also bears irrefutable testimony to the horror of that battle, the bloodiest of the Civil War, and to the sacrifice of the more than fifty thousand men during four days in the summer of 1863.

The Landmarks of American History series has emerged from this belief in the power of place to move us and to teach us. It was with this same philosophy in mind that in 1966 Congress authorized the establishment of the National Register of Historic Places, "the Nation's official list of cultural resources worthy of preservation." These enduring symbols of the American experience are as diverse as the immigration station on Angel Island in San Francisco Bay, which served as U.S. entry point for thousands of Asian immigrants; or Sinclair Lewis's Boyhood Home in Sauk Centre, Minnesota, the place that inspired the novelist's Nobel Prize-winning descriptions of small-town America; or the Cape Canaveral Air Force Station in Florida, launch site of Neil Armstrong's historic trip to the moon. Taken together, such places define us as a nation.

The historic sites presented in this series are selected from the National Register, and they are more than interesting places. The books in this series are written by some of our finest historians—based at universities, historic museums, and historic sites—all nationally recognized experts on the central themes of their respective volumes. For them, historic sites are not just places to visit on a field trip, but primary sources that inform their scholarship. Not simply illustrations of history, they bring the reality of our past to life, making it meaningful to our present and useful for our future.

How to Use This Book

This book is designed to tell the story of American history from a unique perspective: the places where it was made. Each chapter profiles a historic site listed on the National Register of Historic Places, and each site is used as the centerpiece for discussion of a particular aspect of history—for example, Independence Hall for the Declaration of Independence, or the Woolworth store in the Downtown Greensboro Historic District for Martin Luther King Jr.'s role in the civil rights movement. This book is not intended as an architectural history; it is an American history.

On page 6 (opposite the table of contents), there is a regional map of the United States locating each of the main sites covered in this volume. Each chapter in this volume contains a main essay that explains the site's historical importance; a fact box (explained below); and one or two maps that locate the site in the region or show its main features. Each chapter also contains a box listing sites related to the main subject. For each related site, the box includes the official name, address, phone, website, whether it is a National Historic Landmark (NHL) or part of the National Park Service (NPS), and a short description. As much as possible, the author has selected related sites that are geographically diverse and open to the public.

Many of the chapters feature primary sources related to the thematic discussion. These include, for example, letters, journal entries, legal documents, and newspaper articles. Each primary source is introduced by an explanatory note or a caption, indicated by the symbol ☥.

At the back of the book is a timeline of important events mentioned in the text, along with a few other major events that help give a chronological context for the book's theme. A list of further reading includes site-specific reading, along with general reading pertinent to the book.

Fact Boxes

Each chapter has a fact box containing reference information for its main site. This box includes a picture of the site; the site's official name on the National Register;

contact information; National Register Information System number (which you can you use to obtain more details about the site from the National Register, whose contact information appears at the back of this book); whether the site is a National Historic Landmark (NHL) or part of the National Park Service (NPS); and important dates, people, and events in the site's history.

Acts of Congress recognize and protect America's 386 National Park Service units, including National Parks, National Historic Sites, National Historic Battlefields, and National Monuments. The Secretary of the Interior designates National Historic Landmarks, of which there are more than 2,300. States, federal agencies, and Indian tribes have nominated the majority of the seventy-five thousand properties listed in the National Register of Historic Places, some of which are also historic units of the National Park Service and National Historic Landmarks.

Picture of site ———

Official site name ———
Valley Forge National Historic Park

Contact information ———
Valley Forge, PA 19482
610-783-1077

Website ———
www.nps.gov/vafo

National Register Information System number ———
NRIS 66000657

Site is a National Historic Landmark/
National Park Service owns or maintains site ——
NHL/NPS

DATE OF ENCAMPMENT
Date built or other significant dates ———
Winter 1777–78

ORIGINAL OWNER
Architect, builder, or original owner ———
Laetitia Penn, daughter of Pennsylvania's founder, William Penn

SIGNIFICANCE
Summary of site's significance ———
At Valley Forge Washington's army struggled to keep warm, overcame a poorly organized supply system, and summoned up the discipline and courage to renew fighting when spring arrived. The winter encampment became a test of the army's ability to survive, and therefore a test of the nation's as well.

Preface

The American Revolution is one of the epic events of modern world history, for it marked the independence of thirteen British colonies in North America, established a republic based on principles of self-government that have been copied around the world, and laid down agendas for reform that are still being implemented today. No one who lived through the revolutionary era was untouched by the momentous events of the years from the early 1760s through the conclusion of the war in 1783.

For a long time, Americans were surprisingly indifferent to the key landmarks of the American Revolution. In 1812, Benjamin Franklin's family demolished the beautiful house he built in Philadelphia to prepare the site for division into small building lots. Four years later, Independence Hall was nearly sold to developers who wanted to raze the building and sell the land for commercial development. The pell-mell development of Boston in the nineteenth century wiped out most of the historic buildings associated with the beginning of the American Revolution. Only last-minute efforts saved Jefferson's Monticello and Washington's Mount Vernon when it appeared they would go under the gavel.

The business of restoring, recreating, and immortalizing the landmarks of the American Revolution began in the 1840s, but proceeded only fitfully as the burgeoning nation raced west and the seaport towns of the eastern seaboard mushroomed into vast immigrant-filled industrial centers after the Civil War. Preserving these landmarks took money, influence, time, and intense commitment. Citizens who wanted to preserve and cherish the past were opposed by other citizens, with plenty of money, influence, and commitment of their own, who wanted foremost to build for the future.

Moreover, many Americans thought that obliterating old buildings and paving over old battlefields was a way of freeing themselves from the tyranny of their ancestors. Coming in 1848 to Carpenters Hall in Philadelphia, where the First Continental Congress had met, the historian Benson J. Lossing found a shabby auction house on the first floor and the second floor ringing "with the din of urchins conning over their tasks." "What a desecration!" sputtered Lossing.

> If sensibility is shocked with this outward pollution, it is overwhelmed with indignant shame on entering the hall where . . . the godfathers of our republic convened to stand as sponsors at the baptism of infant American Liberty, to find it filled with every species of merchandise.

The outrage of Lossing and others finally sparked an interest in preservationism and awakened an understanding that while history is about the past, it is for the future. Patriotic preservationist associations such as the Daughters of the American Revolution gathered momentum in the late nineteenth century. In the twentieth century, the National Park Service (NPS), entering a period of growth and influence, assumed a leading role in preserving these historic sites. Many of the landmarks visited in this book are now operated by the NPS, whose painstaking research and restoration projects have peeled away many layers of modification to restore eighteenth-century buildings to their original state.

The landmarks of the American Revolution presented in this book have been selected to help the reader appreciate the multi-faceted nature of the American Revolution and the revolutionary experiences and engagement of women, African Americans, Loyalists, Native Americans, allies from overseas, and figures on the homefront such as religious leaders, artists, and musicians, as well as the more familiar political and military leaders.

Each chapter of this book has a theme. For example, one chapter whose theme is "religion and revolution" brings together religious sites, such as Boston's Old South Meetinghouse, and the revolutionaries who used them to show how importantly religion figured in the revolutionary movement. Interpretation of the main site in each chapter carries forward the story; but secondary and related sites have been selected in order to show how the Revolution occurred over a vast, geographically diverse terrain where people mixed, quilt-like, in a variety of patterns. Together, the many sites portrayed in this book will take the reader back more than 200 years to savor and see physical remains of the nation's birth.

Lexington Green

Lexington, Mass.

The Road to Revolution

In militiaman Ralph Earl's drawing of the fight at Lexington Green, the village meetinghouse and tavern appear in the background. The militiamen are fleeing their fallen compatriots in the foreground as the mounted Major John Pitcairn gives the order to fire.

S tand your ground! Don't fire unless fired upon! But if they want to have a war, let it begin here!" These were the steely words of Captain John Parker, commanding officer of the militia of Lexington, Massachusetts, at dawn on April 19, 1775. Alerted by Paul Revere and William Dawes of the approaching British Regulars, about seventy sleepy "minutemen"—farmers and artisans from the town who had been training for a war that seemed imminent— assembled in Lexington on the rough, pasturelike village green called "the common." The green itself had been the common property of all town residents since 1711, when they raised funds to create a village common. Soon the British troops arrived, having marched through the night from Boston for five hours. They were led by Major John Pitcairn, commander of the Royal Marines. Their mission was to seize arms and ammunition stored

in Concord, seven miles west of Lexington. They also hoped to surprise John Hancock and Samuel Adams, leaders of the patriot resistance to British policies, and march these two Boston stalwarts back to the city, where they would be questioned and possibly charged with treason.

Facing the minutemen on the rough Lexington common, dotted with clumps of untended brush, a red-coated officer shouted: "Lay down your arms, you damned rebels, and disperse." Most of the muttering militiamen began to leave. Then a shot rang out. Without orders, the nervous British troops began firing on the farmers and village artisans. The retreating Americans left Lexington Green stained with blood, with eight of their men dead and nine wounded. One British soldier was wounded.

These were the opening shots of the American Revolution. When the British troops moved on to Concord, they found no munitions (which the patriots had carefully hidden) and warily eyed the freshly arrived Massachusetts militia units who took up positions in the hills outside the town. When the British set fire to the courthouse, the militia attempted to cross North Bridge and drive the redcoats from Concord. In the ensuing battle, the Massachusetts men held their ground, fought effectively, and drove the redcoats from Concord in disorder. The British soldiers retreated to Boston, a journey that took them the remainder of that long day.

The British retreat moved eastward past the Lexington Green, and along the way, Captain Parker's men took their revenge for their bloody losses on the town common. Firing from cover along a narrow road, the minutemen from Lexington and a dozen other eastern Massachusetts villages attacked again and again, scattering the reeling enemy. The British were saved only by the arrival of reinforcements from Boston. Before the day was over, the Americans killed or wounded 273 British soldiers while suffering 95 casualties—49 killed and 46 wounded. The fact that citizen-soldiers could face and even defeat trained, professional troops was as fortifying for the patriots as it was discouraging to the British. Years later, when asked why he faced the professional British regulars, Levi Preston replied: "We had always governed ourselves and we always meant to. [The British] didn't mean that we should."

Only twenty-five years old at the time, Daniel Chester French, a native of Concord, created The Minuteman *in 1875 to mark the centennial of the skirmish. The citizen-soldier holds a musket in his right hand while his left hand rests on the handle of his plow.*

Finally the British arrived in Boston, but their humiliation was not over. They had already marched more than twenty miles and now, exhausted and consumed with thirst, they confronted militia units pouring in from all directions. "The rebels were in great numbers," Lord Percy, a British officer, remembered, "the whole country having collected for twenty miles around." Panicked and out of ammunition, six British soldiers surrendered to an elderly woman who was digging weeds from a vacant field. Delivering the soldiers to an American militia captain, she lectured the stricken redcoats: "If you ever live to get back, you tell King George that an old woman took six of his grenadiers prisoner."

Nearly fifteen months would pass before the Americans declared independence, but the skirmishes at Lexington Green and Concord were the beginning of a war that continued until 1783. Bottling up the British in Boston, a large militia army cut off all provisions from the countryside, quickly putting the encircled British on salt rations. One of the militiamen, twenty-two-year-old Lemuel Haynes, born of a white mother and enslaved African father, wrote out a long ballad on what he had witnessed after marching with his townsmen from

After Parliament passed the Stamp Act in 1764, many documents had to bear this stamp. In most cities, men appointed as the stamp distributors found themselves candidates for tarring and feathering by angry colonists.

Granville on April 19, 1775. Titling his poem "The Battle of Lexington," Haynes, who later would become the first black minister to Congregational churches of New England, wrote:

> The Nineteenth Day of April last
> We shall ever retain
> As monumental of the past
> most bloody shocking Scene
>
> Then Tyrants fill'd with horrid Rage
> A fatal Journey went
> & Unmolested to engage
> And slay the innocent . . .
>
> At Lexington they did appear
> Array'd in hostile Form
> And tho our Friends were peacefull there
> Yet on them fell the Storm. . . .
>
> With Sword & Arms they now begun
> The Conflict to decide
> And Blood in great Effusion run
> From ev'ry wounded Side . . .
>
> For Liberty, each Freeman Strives
> As it's a Gift of God
> And for it willing yield their Lives
> And Seal it with their Blood
>
> This Motto may adorn their Tombs
> (Let tyrants come and view)
> "We rather seek these silent Rooms
> Than live as Slaves to You"

The skirmish at Lexington Green was not the cause of the American Revolution. It was only the last of a long string of tense events that brought the American colonies into sharp conflict with the mother country and led finally to the Declaration of Independence in July 1776 in Philadelphia. New England, particularly Massachusetts, had been at the storm center in the disputes over new British colonial policies that erupted after Parliament passed the detested Stamp Act in 1764, which imposed taxes on newspapers, legal documents, diplomas, and even dice.

Boston was the center of Massachusetts protests, with Stamp Act riots in August 1764 all but demolishing the houses of Stamp Distributor Andrew Oliver and Lieutenant Governor Thomas Hutchinson. From that point on, the

Lexington Green

Massachusetts Avenue,
  Harrington Road, and
  Bedford Street
Lexington, MA 02173

NRIS No. 66000767
NHL

SIGNIFICANCE
At Lexington Green, on the morning of April 19, 1775, minutemen of the Massachusetts militia fought with British forces in a skirmish that initiated the Revolutionary War.

challenge was to spread revolutionary fervor to the surrounding countryside and throughout the thirteen colonies. Key milestones along the road to war were the Boston Massacre of 1770, where British soldiers fired on taunting roughnecks; the Boston Tea Party of 1773, when Bostonians dressed as Native Americans threw barrels of tea arriving on a merchant ship into the harbor; and the subsequent closing of the Boston port by the British and the dismissal of the colonial legislature in 1774.

While the devastated British Regulars licked their wounds after reaching Boston after sundown on April 19, 1775, the American leaders immediately began to publicize the battles at Lexington Green and Concord. Now they needed to rouse the rest of the colonies, to

Whipping up Revolutionary Spirit with Political Cartoons

The minutemen on Lexington Green fought with their guns, but others fought with their pens. Paul Revere, closely connected with the battles at Concord and Lexington, created images intended to fuel the revolutionary cause. In England, some illustrators were sympathetic to the American cause, although the message of the cartoon shown here was ambiguous.

The Boston scene portrays the tarring and feathering of John Malcolm, one of the king's customs officers, whom most Bostonians hated for his frequent informing on smugglers avoiding the customs duties. Snared by a crowd in January 1774, just a few weeks after Bostonians had dumped a shipload of tea into Boston harbor, Malcolm was subjected to the painful ritual of being stripped, having hot tar poured on his naked body, and finally being coated with goose feathers. A tar-and-feathering victim was usually carted around town or made to sit on the gallows until he repented his "crime." Here a noose hangs from the Liberty Tree, an ancient elm and familiar landmark that stood near the causeway leading from Boston to Cambridge, the route taken by

the British forces marching to Lexington Green. When bringing food into the city by this road, farmers were politicized in the years after 1764 by seeing effigies of the English king's advocates hanging from this tree.

In this cartoon, "The Bostonians Paying the Excise-man, or Tarring & Feathering," gleeful Bostonians pour tea down British customs officer John Malcolm's throat. Tacked upside down on the Liberty Tree is a copy of the hated Stamp Act.

convince them that Massachusetts' war was the struggle of all thirteen colonies. Immediately they dispatched seasoned horsemen who galloped to Connecticut and points southward. Within two days, all of Connecticut heard about what Boston doctor Joseph Warren called "an early, true, and authentick account of this inhuman proceeding." New Yorkers had the news by April 23 and Philadelphians a day later.

Meanwhile, patriot printers were busy at their presses, and the blood-soaked grass at Lexington's common played an important role. From Worcester, Massachusetts, Isaiah Thomas was running his *Massachusetts Spy* with a masthead motto: "Americans! Liberty or Death! Join or Die!" Also pressed into action was Ralph Earl, a common soldier with artistic ability. Massachusetts leaders pulled him from the ranks and commissioned him to make sketches that could be used to burn the scenes at Lexington Green and Concord into the consciousness of colonists hundreds of miles away. Before making his drawings, Earl interviewed survivors and walked over the sites of the action. He faithfully rendered the terrain, the nearby buildings, and the general positioning of the British Regulars and Massachusetts militiamen. However, the scene he portrayed, showing British Regulars firing into the backs of presumably innocent Lexington farmers mainly trying to flee, was calculated propaganda. Colonial leaders quickly turned Earl's drawings into copperplate

Ezekiel Russell printed this broadside in Salem as part of the campaign to radicalize the countryside after the Lexington-Concord firefights. Each coffin is labeled with the name of a fallen citizen. Russell added more coffins in later editions after some of the wounded had died.

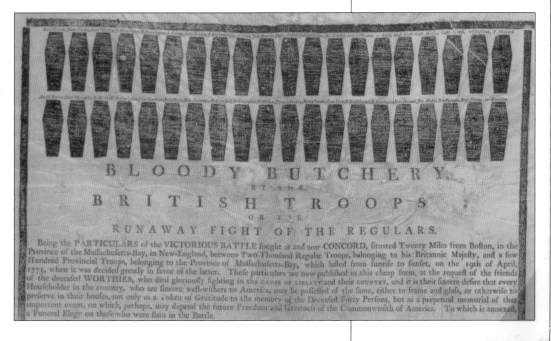

engravings from which hundreds of prints were made. Thus they spread the idea that the colonists were faultless in protesting imperial policies since the Stamp Act crisis of 1764.

Broadsides (printed sheets suitable for posting on tavern doors and lampposts) sermons, and newspapers replaced muskets and bayonets for most of the next year. In this paper war, the memory of Lexington Green was carefully cultivated as the Continental Congress, meeting in Philadelphia, haltingly made the decision to turn an undeclared war into a declaration of independence.

Lexington Green got a facelift in the late nineteenth century when Lexington villagers transformed it from a casually maintained open space for common use into a monumental park commemorating the martyrs of April 19, 1775. Triangular in shape, Lexington Green now features several monuments. Villagers had erected a granite obelisk in 1799 to commemorate those who died in the battle. Seven were buried in the tomb beneath the monument in 1835 after their bodies were disinterred from the Old Burying Ground nearby. More evocative is

Riding an average of seventy miles a day, Paul Revere carried copies of the Suffolk Resolves to Philadelphia protesting Parliament's Intolerable Acts of 1774. The town of Boston reimbursed this early Pony Express rider for his travel expenses.

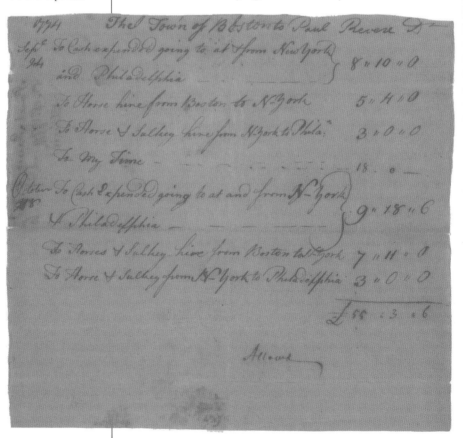

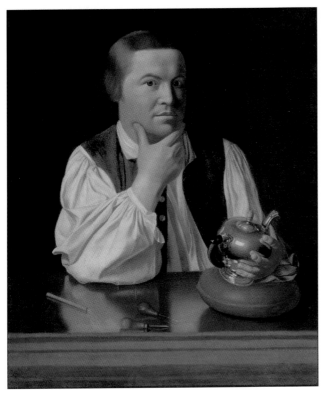

Boston's John Singleton Copley painted the young Paul Revere just a few years before the Lexington Green skirmish. Proud of his craft skills, Revere had himself portrayed in his craftsman clothes with his silversmith's tools lying on the table and his left hand cradling a just-completed teapot.

a life-size bronze figure of a colonial farmer cradling his musket, erected in 1900 when patriotic organizations worked to preserve historic sites connected to the American Revolution. Today, thousands of history buffs from Canada, England, and the United States reenact the battle that followed the Lexington Green confrontation, when minutemen drove British soldiers from Concord's Old North Bridge.

Lexington Green is now a national icon, a symbol of a citizen army fighting for rights they insisted they had acquired at birth. The Lexington Green was larger in 1775 than it is today. The installation of modern roads has reduced its size. The Buckman Tavern by the Green, a popular gathering place at the time, still stands today, and the Meeting House, one of what the New England Puritans called a "Lord's barn," continues to look over the green. At the time of the American Revolution, the green was more of a cow pasture than the smoothly graded, carefully tended land now visited so frequently as a national shrine and trod upon as hallowed ground.

PAUL REVERE HOUSE

19 North Square
Boston, MA 02113
617-523-2338
www.paulreverehouse.org

Revere's clapboard house, with its distinctive diamond-shaped leaded window panes, is the oldest house in downtown Boston and one of the few survivors from the colonial era.

Paul Revere's house stands on North Square in Boston's densely packed North End, just a few blocks from the waterfront that was dotted with wharves and warehouses in the colonial era. Settled by the families of shipwrights, barrel makers, sailors, tavern keepers, sail makers, and shopkeepers, the North End was where many of the clamorous protests against English policies.

Revere's house is one of the few in this city of crooked streets and narrow alleys to survive from the eighteenth century. Revere purchased the weather-blackened clapboard house with its striking diamond-shaped windowpanes in 1770 and lived there in 1775 with his second wife and their seven children. His ride through the night to alert the colonists that the British were marching into the countryside to seize Sam Adams and John Hancock as traitors and to confiscate patriot munitions made Revere famous throughout the colonies. Riding Brown Beauty, a mare of great strength borrowed from John Larkin, a deacon of Charlestown's congregational church, Revere galloped 20 miles or more out of the hill-covered Boston peninsula and across the narrow isthmus called Boston Neck to reach his destination. A British patrol captured Revere but released him within a few hours. But the British kept Brown Beauty, preventing Revere from completing his ride.

Living in Boston's North End put Revere in the thick of radical politics, although he was more moderate than many of his friends. North End residents had been avid participants in the Stamp Act Riots of 1764, when they nearly demolished the houses of Thomas Hutchinson and Andrew Oliver and terrorized other royal officials. The Boston Massacre of 1770 occurred in King Street, only a few minutes from Revere's house, and the house was but a minute to the wharves, where Revere was one of the main leaders of the Tea Party in 1773.

For an urban dweller, Revere was an accomplished horseman. A year before his famous midnight ride, he had carried the Suffolk Resolves to Philadelphia, where the Continental Congress was sitting. The Resolves proclaimed England's "Intolerable Acts" of 1774 (closing the port of Boston, curtailing the city's beloved town meetings, and dismissing the colony's legislature) to be against England's constitution. He made the 350-mile trip on rough roads in five days. Four other times he rode to New York or Philadelphia as courier and emissary of Boston's Committee of Correspondence, a key organizer of resistance strategies.

Revere's house became a teeming tenement in the nineteenth century when Irish immigrants crowded into Boston. Many decades later, from 1906 to 1908, the Paul Revere Memorial Association restored the house and opened it as a tourist attraction. Today it is surrounded by modern buildings of glass, steel, and concrete, leaving the visitor to imagine the horse-and-cart-filled narrow streets of Revere's Boston. His dwelling is the only Revolutionary War structure on the Freedom Trail, the National Park Service's self-guided tour of Boston's revolutionary sites.

BUNKER HILL MONUMENT

Breed's Hill
Charlestown, MA 02129
www.nps.gov/bost
NHL/NPS

On June 17, 1775, two months after the Lexington and Concord conflicts, the first full-scale battle occurred on Breed's Hill across the Charles River from Boston in Charlestown. In the dead of night, 1,200 New England militiamen, many of whom had also fought at Lexington and Concord, constructed a redoubt, a fortified entrenchment, from which they hoped to dislodge the British troops occupying Boston. Bunker Hill was the intended redoubt, but in their haste the militia dug into the smaller Breed's Hill nearby. At daylight, the British reacted swiftly. Two assaults by British infantry fell back before withering patriot fire, but a third succeeded. The Americans sustained more than 400 casualties; the British lost far more, nearly half of their 2,200 troops. "If we have eight more such victories," one Englishman ruefully remarked, "there will be nobody left to bring the news." Nine months later, with General George Washington in charge of a Continental Army positioned outside Boston, the British abandoned the city.

A 221-foot obelisk commemorating the battle rises above a four-acre park. At the base of the monument stands a statue of Colonel William Prescott, who commanded the American soldiery from Massachusetts, Connecticut, and Rhode Island. Construction on the obelisk began in 1825, but it took seventeen years to complete and dedicate the granite structure.

SCOTCHTOWN (PATRICK HENRY HOME)

16120 Chiswell Lane
Beaverdam, VA 23015
804-227-3500
NHL

From 1771 to 1777, while he played a major role in leading the colonies into war against the British, the Virginia planter Patrick Henry lived in a large frame house in Scotchtown, Virginia. At nearly 100 feet long, Henry's house was one of Virginia's largest. Fireplaces served by two massive chimneys heated the house. The basement alone contained eight rooms and a wine cellar. The Henry house was extensively remodeled after its acquisition by the Taylor family in 1832. The new owners razed the original two chimneys and replaced them with four new ones. Modern restoration of the mansion and its outbuildings has been in progress since 1958 when the Association for the Preservation of Virginia Antiquities purchased the property.

Rebelling Americans had no hope of securing their independence without unifying the southern, mid-Atlantic, and New England colonies, and Henry was instrumental in tying Virginia's fate to that of Massachusetts. A leader of the radical opposition to British policies, he served as a Virginia delegate to the Continental Congress. In 1775, he exhorted the Virginia revolutionary convention: "There is no retreat but in submission and slavery! Our chains are forged. Their clanking may be heard on the plains of Boston. The war is inevitable—and let it come!"

Most of the fighting during the battle of Bunker Hill actually took place on Breed's Hill, where this 221-foot granite monument to the Battle of Bunker Hill is located.

Independence Hall, Independence National Historical Park

Philadelphia, Pa.

Declaring Independence

In this interior of Independence Hall as it appeared in 1856, after much restoration, a bald eagle sculpture is perched atop the Liberty Bell while a marble statue of George Washington gazes at it. On the wall are portraits of Revolutionary-era leaders, most of them painted by Charles Willson Peale.

T his morning is assigned for the greatest debate of all," noted John Adams, a Massachusetts delegate to the Second Continental Congress, which was meeting in the Pennsylvania State House in Philadelphia on July 1, 1776. At the end of that day, the delegates from nine of the thirteen colonies rose from the long table in the handsomely paneled room to vote for the Declaration of Independence. The delegates of two colonies voted against the Declaration, written by a committee chaired by Thomas Jefferson; another delegation split its vote; and a fourth abstained. John Hancock, president of Congress, urged unanimity: "There must be no pulling different ways; we must all hang together." Benjamin Franklin concurred: "We must indeed all hang together, or most assuredly we shall all hang separately."

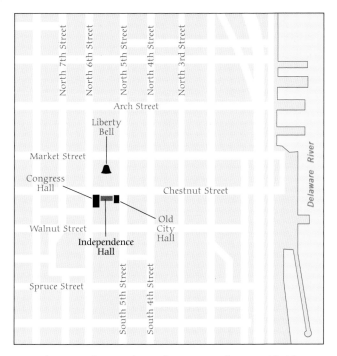

The next day, twelve colonies voted yes, with New York's delegation abstaining. On July 4, Congress sent the Declaration of Independence to the printer. Four days later, Philadelphians thronged the shrub-dotted State House yard to hear it read aloud. They cheered the reading by Philadelphia's sheriff that "these United Colonies are, and of right ought to be, free and independent States." Then they tore the king's coat of arms from above the State House door and later that night, amid more cheers, toasts, and clanging church bells, hurled this symbol of more than a century and a half of colonial dependency on English rule into a roaring bonfire.

Cherished today by millions of visitors each year, Independence Hall was not known by that name for a long time. Rather it opened as the Pennsylvania State House in 1756, when the American colonies were firmly attached to England. Construction of the hall began in 1732 on a gently sloping piece of land five blocks from the Delaware River on the outskirts of the small seaport town, where visiting Native Americans had earlier camped.

As was typical in the British colonies, amateur architect Andrew Hamilton, one of Philadelphia's most prominent lawyers and speaker of the colony's representative assembly, sketched a two-story brick building with clean lines and a symmetry reflecting the eighteenth-century English embrace of Italian Renaissance architecture, particularly that of sixteenth-century architect Andrea Palladio. Palladio believed that architectural beauty rested on the harmony of the component parts of a building. Although the style became known as Georgian, after King George I, the design of the building followed Palladio's three-part arrangement of a central building flanked by wings that were attached to the main structure by covered arched walks, or piazzas. Hamilton sketched four large windows on either side of a great front door and an elegant cupola reminiscent of the one at Gray's Inn Hall in London, where he had studied law.

Working from Hamilton's sketch, Philadelphia's master carpenter Edmund Woolley supervised a large crew of workers—carpenters, stone cutters, brick makers, masons, glaziers, painters, metal workers, and laborers—to construct the building. The hall took twenty-four years to complete, and some of the laborers spent most of their careers on its construction. Even before it was finished, a visiting Swedish botanist, Peter Kalm, called it "a fine, large building having a tower with a bell, and . . . the greatest ornament in the town."

Inside the building's first floor, on either side of a central hall, were two forty-square-foot chambers with ceilings twenty feet high. On the second floor, the interior space was divided lengthwise into halves, one used to create a single room running the entire length of the 107-foot-long building and the other divided into two large rooms. All business of the colony, in the hands of the Assembly, the Council, and the Supreme Court, was conducted in this State House. One of its wings lodged visiting Native American delegations. The State House also hosted meetings of the American Philosophical Society,

The Pennsylvania State House, later destined to become Independence Hall, was first portrayed on the large "Map of Philadelphia and Parts Adjacent," published in Philadelphia in 1752.

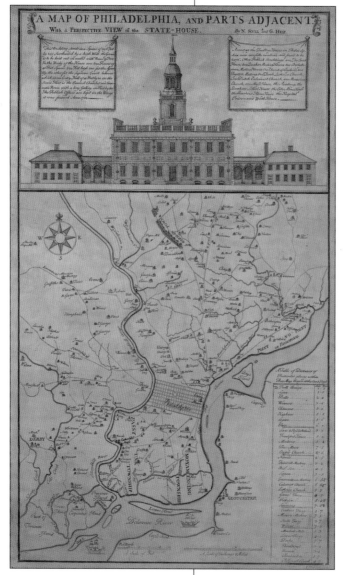

the first scientific and intellectual organization formed in the American colonies; anatomy lectures by the city's eminent doctors; and fancy banquets and balls celebrating the king's birthday or victories in Britain's Seven Years War with France, which lasted from 1756 to 1763. Its yard, later enclosed with a seven-foot brick wall, was also the main site in Philadelphia for casting votes and a gathering place for the public to hear speeches from colonial politicians.

Throughout the Revolution, the State House hummed with the activities not only of the Continental Congress but also the government of Pennsylvania. Elected representatives in each body mingled in the State House, in the streets outside it, in the nearby taverns, and in the salons of wealthy Philadelphians. There Pennsylvanians met Virginians for the first time; Connecticut men rubbed elbows with Georgians; Rhode Islanders dined with Carolinians. In June 1775, in the Assembly Room where Congress met, the delegates appointed George Washington as commander in chief of the newly authorized Continental Army. Another thirteen months later, on July 15, 1776, delegates from every Pennsylvania county—many of them farmers and artisans—convened here to draft a constitution for Pennsylvania. In 1779, Pennsylvania legislators drafted the first state law abolishing slavery, although gradually.

Two years into the war, the State House suffered all the indignities of an occupying army. When the British defeated the Americans at Brandywine, southwest of the city, the Continental Congress and state governments fled, hauling off the State House bell (better known today as the Liberty Bell) to Allentown to keep the British from melting it into metal for ammunition. When British troops led by General William Howe occupied the city between September 1777 and June 1778, the first floor of the State House became a hospital and its second floor a jail for American officers. The dead carried from its bloodied chambers were buried in the Strangers' Burial Ground diagonally behind the State House or were thrown into an open pit dug just outside the building. When the British evacuated the city, they left behind a building "in a most filthy condition and the inside torn much to pieces," according to Josiah Bartlett, a member of the Continental Congress. So foul was the air inside the State House that the returning delegates to the

Independence Hall, Independence National Historical Park

Chestnut Street, between Fifth
   and Sixth Streets
Philadelphia, PA 19106
215-597-8974
www.nps.gov/inde

NRIS 66000683
NPS

DATE BUILT
1732–56

ARCHITECT
Andrew Hamilton

SIGNIFICANCE
Independence Hall, called the Pennsylvania State House at the time of the American Revolution, was the site where the second Continental Congress met; where the Declaration of Independence was drafted, debated, and signed; and where members of the Constitutional Convention of 1787 met to construct and sign the Federal Constitution.

Continental Congress had to meet elsewhere until the building was scrubbed down from top to bottom.

Better times returned to the State House after the British withdrew, but it sometimes became a place of protest as well as a site for celebration. Here Philadelphians rushed in October 1781 to celebrate news of Lord General Charles Cornwallis's surrender at Yorktown to Washington's army and his French auxiliaries. Less than two years later, angry Pennsylvanian soldiers surrounded the State House and demanded back pay so vociferously that the Continental Congress fled to the sleepy town of Princeton, never to return to Philadelphia. In 1787, fifty-five delegates from twelve states redignified the old State House when they arrived to spend a hot, muggy summer there writing the Constitution that the states would ratify in the next year. Pennsylvania's ratifying convention met in the State House for several weeks in 1788, and two years later a state convention met there to revise Pennsylvania's constitution. On its heels, the U.S. Congress arrived from

John Adams Writes to His Wife about Signing the Declaration of Independence

 John Adams, one of the Massachusetts delegates to the Second Continental Congress, was a leader in moving the Congress toward accepting the Declaration of Independence. On July 3, 1776, Adams fervently wrote his wife Abigail about the vote of twelve colonies for independence—only New York abstained—in the Assembly Room of what would become known as Independence Hall.

Yesterday the greatest question was decided which ever was decided in America, and a greater, perhaps, never was nor will be decided among men. [Britain had been] filled with folly, and America with wisdom; at least this is my judgment. Time must determine. It is the will of Heaven that the two countries should be sundered forever.... [Independence day will be observed as a holiday,] the most memorable epoch in the history of America [and] will be celebrated by succeeding generations as the great anniversary festival.... [It should be commemorated by] a solemn act of devotion to God Almighty.... It ought to be solemnized with pomp and parade, with shows, games, sports, guns, bells, bonfires, and illuminations, from one end of the continent to the other, from this time forward forevermore.

New York in December 1790. It would direct the nation from the State House in Philadelphia for ten years.

In the early nineteenth century, the State House, with its spacious yard, remained the prime site for celebrating the nation's independence and the birthday of its first President, although it was not yet known as Independence Hall. Even before George Washington died in 1799, Philadelphians were gathering around the State House to toast the President, conduct civic feasts, and display illuminations and transparencies honoring the Founding Fathers. Sometimes the civic festivals bordered on what one proper Quaker lady, Elizabeth Drinker, described in her diary in 1798 as "a little mob fashion."

After Congress declared the Fourth of July a national holiday in 1799, it became the nation's principal patriotic celebration. But it took only a few years for Philadelphia's State House yard to yield to "mob fashion"—with grave results. By 1805, Independence Square had become a place not so much to memorialize the past as to lay down a color line. When black Philadelphians came to celebrate the nation's birthday, white roughnecks drove their fellow citizens from the square with a barrage of rocks and curses.

In 1784, English immigrant Robert Pine started a painting of the Second Continental Congress voting for independence, which was completed by Edward Savage in about 1801. The portrayal of the State House Assembly Room is historically accurate.

A few years later, the city's leading African-American sail maker, James Forten, who had fought in the American Revolution as a fifteen-year-old powder boy on Stephen Decatur's warship, wrote bitterly in his *Letters from a Gentleman of Colour,* "Is it not wonderful that the day set apart for the festival of liberty, should be abused by the advocates of freedom, in endeavoring to sully what they profess to adore?" The landmark of American ideals had become a staging ground for racial conflicts. For years thereafter, black Philadelphians would celebrate January 1, the day that the horrific slave trade ended in 1808, rather than July 4, as their Independence Day.

After the war, few people felt inspired to honor the nation's birthplace. In fact, the old State House slowly decayed, especially after the Pennsylvanian government relocated to Lancaster in 1799, and the federal government left Philadelphia for Washington, D.C., the following year. Pennsylvania's legislature had so little regard for what we now esteem as a national shrine that in 1816, seeking money to build a new capitol in Harrisburg, it approved the sale of the State House yard behind the building. The spacious yard, now a restful tree-shaded park in bustling Philadelphia, was to be divided into house lots after streets were run through the yard. The State House itself, along with its now-famous Liberty Bell, was to be sold as surplus property to the highest bidder. In 1802 Charles Willson Peale installed his museum of natural history and curiosities, and his menagerie munched quietly on the State House lawn.

In 1818, the city of Philadelphia came to the rescue of the State House. For $70,000, the city purchased the building and its large yard, but Philadelphians did not truly become interested in the building until 1824. This new affection arose from plans to celebrate the arrival of Marquis de Lafayette, who was on his first visit to the United States since he had fought with the American army nearly a half-century before. Planners for the celebration made the old State House the main site for welcoming the aging French compatriot and rushed to decorate the room where the Declaration of Independence and the Constitution had been drafted, debated, and signed.

Lafayette's visit made it clear that the State House was a precious bridge between the past, the present, and the future. Responding to the mayor's welcome, Lafayette referred to "this hallowed Hall" and to the "Birthplace of Independence," noting that "here within these sacred walls . . . was boldly declared the independence of these United States," and "here was planned the formation of our virtuous, brave, revolutionary army, and the providential inspiration received that gave the command of it to our beloved, matchless Washington." Now this room acquired a new name—the Hall of Independence— and the timeworn State House acquired a new name— Independence Hall. With a new lease on life, Independence Hall was on its way to becoming a national icon.

Thereafter, "Hall of Independence" became the common term for the east room of the State House where the Declaration had been signed, and within a few decades the entire building was commonly referred to as Independence Hall. In 1825, as part of renaming its public squares, Philadelphia officially designated Independence Square. Three years later, the city commissioned the rebuilding of the long-demolished steeple. The restoration of Washington's Mount Vernon, which began in 1858, is widely regarded as the beginning of a national historical preservation movement. However, it was the spirited debate over restoring Independence Hall's steeple to its original form that touched off the desire to preserve historic memory by restoring the historic buildings associated with the American Revolution.

From then until now, money and ingenuity have been lavished on Independence Hall, its associated buildings, and Independence Square. By the 1830s, Independence

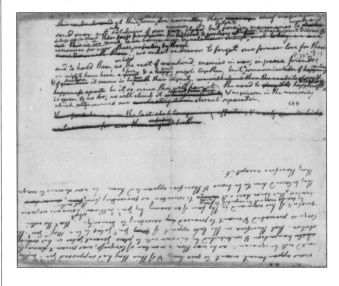

Nobody gets a perfect first draft, as this fragment of the Declaration of Independence written by Thomas Jefferson shows. Some of the revised language in this version was deleted by the Continental Congress.

Slavery and Independence Hall

Holy Bible.
Thou shalt not deliver unto the master his servant which has escaped from his master unto thee. He shall dwell with thee: Even among you in that place which he shall choose in one of thy gates where it liketh **Effects of the Fugitive-Slave-Law.**
Declaration of independence.
We hold that all men are created equal, that they are endowed by their Creator with certain unalienable rights, that among these are life, liberty and the pursuit of happiness.

Independence Hall has been a symbol of American founding principles, including freedom, quality, and justice. Yet it has been a contested place where Americans divided sharply over how fundamental rights would be made operational. This was clear in the 19th century, when the building was no longer Pennsylvania's State House but became the nerve center of Philadelphia's government.

The Compromise of 1850 included a tough new Fugitive Slave law that permitted Southern slave owners or their agents to come north to seize runaway slaves. These alleged fugitives were denied a jury trial; rather, their fate was determined by federal judges or special commissioners. Independence Hall became the scene where accused fugitives were detained in the U.S. Marshal's office, received hearings, and learned their fates.

In 1851, after a Maryland slave owner was killed at a farm in Christiana, near Lancaster,

In this dramatic print published by abolitionists to deplore the Fugitive Slave Act of 1850, six white men fire on ambushed black men in a cornfield.

Pennsylvania, while trying to capture his escaped slaves, several dozen African-American and white "conspirators" were charged with treason for interfering with the Fugitive Slave Law. The prisoners were tried in court on the second floor of the State House. Philadelphians were bitterly divided on the issue. Some agreed with Mr. Aaron of the Pennsylvania Anti-Slavery Society that the black Pennsylvanians at Christiana "were only following the example of Washington and the American heroes of '76." Others rallied at a mass meeting in Independence Square "to prevent the recurrence of so terrible a scene upon the soil of Pennsylvania, to ferret out and punish the murderers." If Independence Hall was becoming sacred ground, it also remained a contested ground.

Hall became a symbolically rich venue for President Andrew Jackson to receive visitors. By 1848, when the body of John Quincy Adams arrived in Philadelphia in transit from Washington to Massachusetts, Independence Hall became for the first time a place for a former President to lie in state, at least for one night. During the Civil War it became a Union shrine, a place to mourn fallen sons, celebrate Union victories, and view the casket of the U.S. President and commander in chief, Abraham Lincoln, after his assassination in April 1865.

The reincarnation of Independence Hall as a consecrated shrine was hastened by Philadelphia's preparations for the Centennial Exposition of 1876—the 100th birthday of independence. The exposition, situated in Fairmount Park, looked forward while celebrating a century of industrial progress and technological innovation; but Independence Hall was a secondary site that looked reverently back to the nation's founding. During the several years spent preparing for the Centennial, spirited arguments erupted over just how to commemorate the "spirit of '76." For example, should a portrait of George III be included while Andrew Jackson's likeness was purged?

Everyone agreed that Independence Hall should be restored as much as possible to its original condition. The old first-floor Assembly Room, long used as a multi-subject museum since the days of Charles Willson Peale was transformed into a national museum where visitors could contemplate the authentic historical artifacts from the founding period. This was not the last remake of Independence Hall, but it was the one that set the course for all succeeding attempts to treat the building as a national treasure.

From the time of Lafayette's festive visit to Philadelphia in 1824, Independence Hall became the focus of historical restoration in Philadelphia, and by 1876 the hall had been restored to its approximate appearance during the American Revolution. Congress Hall and the Supreme Court, the two buildings flanking Independence Hall, were restored in 1913 and 1922 respectively under the supervision of the Philadelphia chapter of the American Institute of Architects. But city and private support could not bear the burden of preserving these national icons, especially since they stood, by the 1930s, in a deteriorating neighborhood in the inner city. Thus, in 1942, while World War II was raging, more than fifty

Philadelphia civic and cultural groups formed the Independence Hall Association, which secured congressional establishment and funding for the Independence National Historical Park in 1948.

Three city blocks, between Walnut and Chestnut Streets and from Second to Fifth Streets, comprise the park, along with nearby buildings of great historical importance: the First and Second Banks of the United States, the Philadelphia Exchange, the Todd and Bishop White House, Carpenters' Hall, and Christ Church (the latter two still privately held but operated by the National Park Service rangers under cooperative agreements).

After it was established by Congress in 1950, the National Park Service assumed responsibility for further restorations within the Independence National Historical Park and for talks and tours by park rangers for the millions of visitors each year. The Park Service has carried out extensive research on each building, has undertaken further restoration over the last half-century, and has transformed what had become a blighted area into an urban landscape that evokes William Penn's dream of Philadelphia as "a greene countrey towne."

John Lewis Krimmel, an immigrant from Württemberg, Germany, depicted election day revelry in front of Independence Hall and its flanking buildings in 1815. All classes of people appear in this rare street scene from the period.

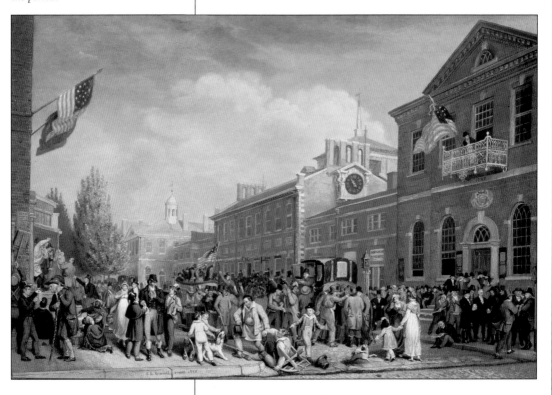

CARPENTERS' HALL

320 Chestnut Street
Philadelphia, PA 19106
215-925-0167
www.nps.gov/inde
NHL/NPS

For seven weeks, beginning on September 5, 1774, the First Continental Congress met in Carpenters' Hall to consider the mounting crisis between Great Britain and its American colonies. In this elegant two-story brick Georgian structure, newly completed in 1774 by the city's master carpenters, the delegates from every colony except Georgia explored each other's views about the series of events that had led to heightened tensions. They also discovered how much they differed on how to respond to the Coercive Acts that had closed the port of Boston and hobbled the Massachusetts provincial government. Here in Carpenters' Hall, the delegates passed a declaration of grievances and resolutions condemning British policies going back to the Stamp Act of 1764, agreed to form a "Continental Association" to boycott imported British goods, and most momentously, agreed that the colonists should take up arms to defend their rights.

Although Carpenters' Hall lost its host role to the State House, just a few blocks away, when the Second Continental Congress arrived in Philadelphia in May 1775, it remained at the hub of the revolution. It served as a military hospital, and Washington's army mounted supply operations from its courtyard. With these military connections, it seemed natural that the War Department moved in when Philadelphia became the nation's capital again in 1790. The First Bank of the United States also moved in and is located there today.

CONGRESS HALL AND OLD CITY HALL

Sixth and Chestnut Streets, Fifth and Chestnut
Streets
Philadelphia, PA 19106
215-597-8974
www.nps.gov/inde
NHL/NPS

The city of Philadelphia began construction of a large county courthouse in 1787 at the southeast corner of Sixth and Chestnut Streets and a new city hall at the southwest corner of Fifth and Chestnut Streets in 1790, both as part of the State House complex. In 1789, the courthouse was ready. The next year, Congress, meeting in New York City, made the decision to move to Philadelphia. With modifications, the county courthouse became Congress Hall, and it was here that the third U.S. Congress met in December. The House of Representatives met on the first floor, where a gallery allowed up to 300 members of the public and the press to judge the quality of their elected legislators. The more august Senate met on the second floor without a gallery. Here, George Washington was inaugurated on March 4, 1793, for his second term as president.

In 1793 Congress Hall was expanded to accommodate a larger House of Representatives. In 1795, carpenters constructed a gallery along one wall of the senate chamber so the public could audit the Senate's deliberations. With the Haitian and French revolutions in full flood, and war in Europe making it difficult for the United States to remain neutral, gallery visitors had plenty to listen to. When construction workers completed the City Hall in 1791, the Supreme Court of the United States, as well as its U.S. District and Circuit courts, preempted the needs of the city. Here, John Jay and Oliver Ellsworth each sat as Chief Justice of the United States in the 1790s.

LIBERTY BELL

Liberty Bell Pavilion, Market Street between
Fifth and Sixth Streets
Philadelphia, PA 19106
215-597-8974
www.nps.gov/inde/liberty-bell.html
NPS

Although most people associate the Liberty Bell with the American Revolution, the bell was cast in London in 1752 and installed the next year in a wooden steeple in the brick tower of the State House in Philadelphia. The bell cracked upon being tested for the first time, and it was recast by two local metalsmiths. It cracked again, according to legend, while tolling in 1835 during funeral observances for U.S. Chief Justice John Marshall.

The bell got its name from its biblical inscription, "Proclaim Liberty Throughout all the Land unto all the Inhabitants Thereof" (Leviticus 25.10). These words inspired colonists through the Revolutionary War years. However, it was not possible to ring the bell for fear that this would collapse the badly deteriorated steeple. In the period before the Civil War, antislavery groups adopted the bell, with its message of freedom for all, as a symbol of their cause. In 1976 the bell was moved from Independence Hall to a nearby glass-walled pavilion erected for the bicentennial year. Plans call for it to move again to a new pavilion at 6th and Market Streets in July 2003.

MONTICELLO

931 Thomas Jefferson Parkway
Charlottesville, VA 22902
434-984-9822
www.monticello.org
NHL

Thomas Jefferson, who wrote the first draft of the Declaration of Independence, which was debated and signed in Independence Hall, constructed his beloved Monticello on the leveled top of a "little mountain," as its name translates. Today, Monticello is one of the most revered and visited shrines of revolutionary America, but for a very long time it was neither cherished nor visited at all. In fact, it was a drag on the real estate market, a neglected and abused building surrounded by ruined gardens and weed-choked fields.

Jefferson designed his mansion when he was a young planter-lawyer; he oversaw its construction by his slaves; and he never stopped remodeling it. Evidence of his fertile mind is

abundant inside and outside Monticello. Inside, visitors see dumbwaiters, disappearing beds, unusual ventilating and lighting contrivances, a duplicate-writing machine, folding doors, steep and narrow staircases hidden in closetlike alcoves (because Jefferson thought staircases were architecturally unattractive), the first swivel chair seen in the United States, and a seven-day clock that runs by weights and pulleys. Outside, they see precisely designed terraced gardens, walks, and subsidiary pavilions. All of it subtly overtakes the visitor. What visitors see at Monticello today is a reconstructed and reassembled complex, the work of a dedicated band of Jefferson worshipers over the last eighty years.

Today, Monticello is one of the most visited historic sites in the United States, and the crowds have kept growing since DNA evidence showed that Jefferson was most likely the father of at least one of the offspring of Sally Hemings, one of Jefferson's several hundred slaves.

Valley Forge National Historic Park

Valley Forge, Pa.

Mobilizing Washington's Army

The March to Valley Forge *was submitted by William B. T. Trego to the Pennsylvania Academy of Fine Arts for a competition in 1883. It remains today one of the most memorable images of Washington's tattered army trudging to winter quarters west of Philadelphia.*

W e had nothing to eat for two or three days previous, except what the trees of the fields and forests afforded us. But we must now have what Congress said, a sumptuous Thanksgiving to close the year of high living we had now nearly seen brought to a close. What do you think it was? . . . each and every man [received] half a gill of rice and a tablespoonful of vinegar.

This is how Private Joseph Plumb Martin, of the Eighth Connecticut Regiment, remembered December 18, 1777, a day of wind and freezing rain. He was among some 11,000 men of George Washington's army, 2,000 without shoes and all of them huddling through the night without tents or bedding. When dawn broke, they began the five-mile march along a rutted road from Gulph Mills, on the Schuylkill River west of Philadelphia, to the Valley Forge encampment. Here in

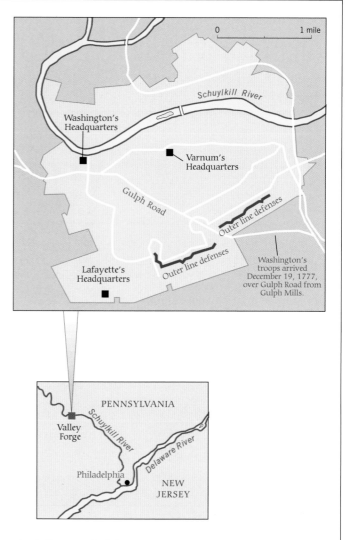

the hilly, wooded farming country settled by Quakers, they would try to regather themselves for the winter near the junction of the Schuylkill River and Valley Creek.

The American deaths in the first year of war—at Lexington and Concord, at Bunker Hill, and especially in the invasion of Canada, where hundreds of colonists died in the fall of 1775 while trying to capture British strongholds at Quebec and Montreal—shocked the rebellious colonists but did not dispirit them. But by the third year of fighting the "spirit of '76" was wearing thin. When the Americans could not prevent the British from occupying the nation's capital of Philadelphia in September 1777, after hard-fought battles at Brandywine and Germantown, the Continental Army had to concentrate on protecting the interior of Pennsylvania from the enemy. All hope for a short war was now dashed. Washington's army withdrew to Valley Forge, eighteen miles west of Philadelphia, while the Continental Congress moved to York, another ninety miles west.

Historic structures and restored earthworks are part of what became the Valley Forge National Historical Park. Congress established the park on July 4, 1976, "to preserve and commemorate for the people of the United States the area associated with the heroic suffering, hardship, and determination and resolve of General George Washington's Continental Army during the winter of 1777–1778."

At the western edge of the 3,466-acre park is Washington's Headquarters, a two-story, three-bay, gable-roofed house built of local fieldstone. The house was constructed in the 1770s by Isaac Potts, a local Quaker

An Ordinary Soldier Remembers the Valley Forge Encampment

 At Revolutionary War historic sites, visitors learn much more about the officers involved than they do about the enlisted soldiers and sailors. No ordinary militiaman could afford to have his portrait painted, and few left behind personal possessions. But a small number wrote down their accounts of the war. One was Joseph Plumb Martin, who joined the military at age fifteen and served for seven years as one of the rare long-term enlistees. Twelve years later, he published his Narrative of Some of the Adventures, Dangers and Sufferings of a Revolutionary Soldier. *His account of arriving at Valley Forge in December 1777 provides a sobering description of Washington's beleaguered army.*

The army was now not only starved but naked. The greatest part were not only shirtless and barefoot but destitute of all other clothing, especially blankets. I procured a small piece of raw cowhide and made myself a pair of moccasins, which kept my feet (while they lasted) from the frozen ground, although . . . the hard edges so galled my ankles while on a march that it was with much difficulty and pain that I could wear them afterwards; but the only alternative I had was to endure this inconvenience or to go barefoot, as hundreds of my companions had to, till they might be tracked by their blood upon the rough frozen ground. . . . Our prospect was indeed dreary. . . . However, there was no remedy, no alternative but this or dispersion [desertion]; but dispersion, I believe, was not thought of-at least I did not think of it. We had engaged in the defense of our injured country and were willing, nay, we were determined to persevere as long as such hardships were not altogether intolerable.

Valley Forge National Historic Park

Valley Forge, PA 19482
610-783-1077
www.nps.gov/vafo

NRIS 66000657
NHL/NPS

DATE OF ENCAMPMENT
Winter 1777–78

ORIGINAL OWNER
Laetitia Penn, daughter of
Pennsylvania's founder,
William Penn

SIGNIFICANCE
At Valley Forge Washington's
army struggled to keep warm,
overcame a poorly organized
supply system, and summoned
up the discipline and courage to
renew fighting when spring
arrived. The winter encampment
became a test of the army's ability
to survive, and therefore a test
of the nation's as well.

ironmaker, who rented it to a widow named Deborah
Hewes in 1777; she sublet it to Washington for the winter encampment. The main section of the house, the
front room that served Washington both as office and
bedroom, is mostly original. From 1975 to 1976, architects restored the kitchen to its approximate configura-
tion during Washington's encampment, using evidence
found in the building's foundation walls to undo much
of the kitchen remodeling of 1840, 1887, and 1933.

In spite of Washington's iconic significance to
Americans, it is the soldiers' huts that spark the most
interest among visitors today. Malnourished and
ill-clothed, the soldiers from eleven colonies built more
than 1,000 cabins, whose logs were held together with
clay with clay. Chopping down trees in the nearby forests
and sawing them into logs and planks, they constructed
twelve-man cabins fourteen feet by sixteen feet, with a
fireplace and chimney at one end and a door of split
oak slabs at the other. Some huts had bark and turf
roofs; others had wooden shake coverings to keep out
the rain. Many soldiers regarded their huts as "tolerably
comfortable," as Washington described them, though
most were poorly heated.

The huts may have kept out snow and rain, but
they couldn't protect against dysentery, typhus, and
typhoid fever, which killed an estimated 1,800 men
before the army broke camp. Among them were African
Americans who served "in abundance" in most regiments,
as the Hessian officer Schloezer noted, and composed
the all-black First Rhode Island Regiment. Many women,
who received pay as cooks, laundresses, seamstresses,
and nurses, also met their deaths at Valley Forge.

Officers fared better at Valley Forge. The David
Stephens House, a nearby farmhouse built in the first
third of the eighteenth century served as the quarters of
General James Mitchell Varnum of Rhode Island. Other
farmhouses were assigned to officers such as Colonel
Daniel Morgan and the Marquis de Lafayette. Lesser
officers occupied larger cabins with fewer inhabitants.
A surgeon from Connecticut, Ebenezer Crosby, claimed
that his hut "afforded much better quarters than you
would imagine, if you consider the materials, season,
and hurry in which it was built."

For the first three months after arriving at Valley
Forge on December 19, 1777, Washington's army spent

most of its time building huts, constructing fortifications, and requisitioning fuel and food. This process was plagued by supply problems—including the willingness of local farmers to sell grain and meat at premium prices to the occupying British army quartered in Philadelphia. Private Martin remembered those first days:

> We were now in a truly forlorn condition—no clothing, no provisions and as disheartened as need be. . . . Our prospect was indeed dreary. In our miserable condition, to go into the wild woods and build us habitations . . . in such a weak, starved and naked condition, was appalling in the highest degree. . . . We then had but little and often nothing to eat for days together; but now we had nothing and saw no likelihood of any betterment to our condition.

A Powder Horn as a Personal Statement

For revolutionary soldiers, the indispensable tools of war were a rifle, a cartridge pouch, and a powder horn. Fashioned from cow or ox horns, powder horns contained the coarse gunpowder used to charge the rifle's muzzle. While in camp, where most soldiers spent the winter months, carving one's powder horn became a popular diversion. Personal statements and decorative motifs carved into powder horns give us unique insights into the sentiments of ordinary soldiers. Powder horns can be seen in museums and displays at most Revolutionary War historic sites.

James Pike, a New England militiaman, carved his version of the Battle of Bunker [Breed's] Hill on June 17, 1775, on his powder horn. Six British soldiers, whom Pike called "Regulars, the Aggressors," are attacking a "Liberty Tree," the New Englanders' symbol of American rights, protected by "Provincials Defending." The powder horn bears this inscription: "JAMES PIKE'S HORN, Made by him at Somersworth, march ye 12th, 1776." In 1833, when he was 80 years old, Pike related in his application for a Revolutionary War pension that "I joined the army at Cambridge [Massachusetts]. . . . I was one of the militia or Provincials as we were then called. . . . I worked all night [at Breed's Hill] digging with a shovel preparing the entrenchments. . . . I was among the last of the Americans that retreated."

The needs of Washington's army, printed on this broadside from August 1775, were huge. One of the complications of supplying the army was that many farmers were also willing to sell to the British army.

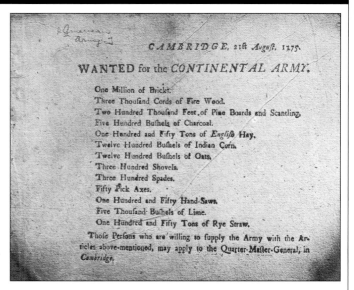

CAMBRIDGE, 21st August, 1775.

WANTED for the CONTINENTAL ARMY.

One Million of Bricks.
Three Thousand Cords of Fire Wood.
Two Hundred Thousand Feet of Pine Boards and Scantling.
Five Hundred Bushels of Charcoal.
One Hundred and Fifty Tons of English Hay.
Twelve Hundred Bushels of Indian Corn.
Twelve Hundred Bushels of Oats.
Three Hundred Shovels.
Three Hundred Spades.
Fifty Pick Axes.
One Hundred and Fifty Hand-Saws.
Five Thousand Bushels of Lime.
One Hundred and Fifty Tons of Rye Straw.

Those Persons who are willing to supply the Army with the Articles above-mentioned, may apply to the Quarter-Master-General, in Cambridge.

Even three months later, on March 20, 1778, the French officer Peter S. DuPonceau remembered "seeing the soldiers popping their heads out of their miserable huts and calling out in an undertone, 'No bread, no soldier!'"

But if the soldiers often went hungry and were ill-clad, they toiled incessantly constructing fortifications against British attack. Designed by a French officer named General Louis Lebeque Duportail, the earthen fortifications constituted an elaborate series of redoubts, or crude forts, and trenches. The outer line fortifications were plowed under after the Revolution when the area returned to farmland, but in recent years they have been carefully rebuilt.

Beginning in March 1778, when the weather moderated, serious training for more effective field maneuvers began. The parade ground now became a prominent feature of the encampment. Although in early February as many as 4,000 men were unavailable for training because they lacked shoes and clothes, the situation improved as spring thaws arrived. In the three months before the army moved out, it underwent a remarkable transformation from a dedicated but poorly trained group to a disciplined professional corps.

Made painfully aware by the public's disregard for their condition that they must survive on their own, Washington's army grew in discipline and morale under the incessant drilling supervised by a Prussian officer, Baron Friedrich von Steuben. The new sense of discipline that von Steuben instilled brought accolades from Washington on down. General Horatio Gates spoke of his "astonishment with which I beheld the order, regularity, and attention, which you have taught the American army; and the obedience, exactness, and true spirit of military discipline, which you have infused into them." Von Steuben also taught the officers not to ride their horses but to trudge with the men. Experiencing the fatigue of twenty-mile marches together bonded the men and their officers. Washington was soon telling his officers that "it ought to be the pride of an officer to share the fatigue as well as danger to which his men are exposed."

As spring progressed, Washington's army not only displayed a renewed discipline and will to fight but heard the happy news that the French had signed a treaty of alliance with the rebelling colonists. Breaking camp on June 19, 1778, Washington's army pursued the British, who had headed north after evacuating Philadelphia. There the Americans engaged them at the Battle of Monmouth Court House in New Jersey with a new martial appearance and revived spirits.

For a long time, the Valley Forge encampment struck no chords of memory. As soon as the army left, nearby farmers swarmed over the site to haul off logs from the cabins to use as split rail fences or housing for livestock and chickens. Returning 10 years later, Washington found "all the works . . . in ruins; and the Incampments in woods where the grounds had not been cultivated." But years later, the winter at Valley Forge came to symbolize American fortitude and courage—the ability to survive extreme deprivation through commitment to a cause. In time, postage stamps and memorabilia burned the image of the Valley Forge winter into the American consciousness.

Baron Friedrich von Steuben drills American units in the snow at Valley Forge. Painted by Edwin Austin Abbey, the work was commissioned for the Pennsylvania State Capitol in Harrisburg.

The kitchen of George Washington's headquarters is filled with a variety of articles from this period. During the winter of 1777–78, the kitchen was rarely this neat and well furnished.

Not until the 1876 Centennial Exposition in Philadelphia, the festive 100th birthday party of the United States that drew millions to what was an international fair, did Valley Forge gain any national attention as a commemorative place. In 1878, a group of local citizens known as the Centennial and Memorial Association raised $3,000 to buy the stone farmhouse that had been Washington's Headquarters and one and one-half acres around it. Formal recognition for his troops who wintered at Valley Forge came when the Pennsylvania legislature designated the area a state park in 1893. The newly formed Valley Forge Park Commission began the acquisition of encampment property and the reconstruction of soldiers' huts, earthworks, buildings, and monuments.

In 1906, the commission purchased Washington's Headquarters from the Centennial Association and incorporated it into the memorial park. At the same time, the commission invited the many states whose regiments composed Washington's army to memorialize sites of their encampment. Valley Forge State Park was the site of huge Boy Scout jamborees in 1950, 1957, and 1964. Those were widely admired events, but thousands of rambunctious Boy Scouts left behind extensive surface and subsurface disturbances. After managing the Valley Forge State Park for eighty-three years, the Park Commission turned it over to the National Park Service in 1976. The Park Service has since carried out further restoration and archaeological research.

WASHINGTON HEADQUARTERS (JACOB FORD, JR., HOUSE)

Juncture of US 202 and NJ 24
Morristown, NJ 07960
973-539-2085
www.nps.gov/morr
NPS

In December 1779, Washington's army limped into a camp four miles southwest of Morristown, New Jersey. There they would spend one of the cruelest winters of the century, one even more miserable than in Valley Forge two years before. Many of the men wore tattered uniforms and huddled for warmth with limited tents for many weeks before they could build crude huts.

Private Joseph Plumb Martin wrote, after a deep snow, of being literally starved for four days when he had not "a single morsel of victuals" except "a little black birch bark which I gnawed off a stick of wood." Although the snow was waist high, guards had to be mounted each day. "As they marched to their different stations," wrote Martin, "they might be traced by the blood of their feet, they were so destitute of shoes and other clothing it seems cruel to drive them out this hard winter." Thus it went during the winter retreat at Morristown, where nearly 11,000 men slowly built a cabin encampment from the forests, regained their strength, reclothed themselves, and prepared for the spring campaign. It was the lowest point of the Revolutionary struggle against Great Britain and the greatest test of Washington's ability to hold his army together.

If his men were as bad off as at Valley Forge, or worse, Washington's accommodations were far better. He directed the army from one of the best houses in Morristown, the large Georgian house of the widow Theodosia Ford, located in the village of several hundred inhabitants. Built in 1772 by Colonel Jacob Ford, Jr., a local mine, forge, and powder mill owner, the house had a symmetrical facade with an impressive main entrance flanked by Ionic columns and ornate cornices. A central hallway ran the length of the house on both the first and second floors. A wing at the east end of the mansion contained the kitchen, pantry, and servants' quarters.

For the seven months that her house became the military headquarters of Washington's Continental Army, the widow Ford and her four children squeezed into two first-floor rooms. The remaining rooms housed Washington's military staff, slaves, and servants. Martha Washington came to spend some of the bone-chilling winter weeks with her husband.

Throughout the winter, Washington and his aides wrestled with the daily problem of supplying food and clothing for the troops; dealt with desertions and the repeated attempts of the soldiers to improve their lot by marauding the countryside; implored the Continental Congress to provide the finances without which the army must surely perish; and—to relieve the dreadful winter conditions and lowered spirits—sought ways to provide entertainment through song and musical performances.

In 1873, the Ford House was rescued from decay and demolition by four patriotic New Jerseyans who purchased the house at auction for $25,000. Over the years they collected historical relics, eventually resulting in an invaluable cache of artifacts and a research library on the revolutionary era with 20,000 books and 50,000 manuscripts. In 1933, the several thousand acres where the soldiers made their winter camp, along with the Ford mansion and the associated buildings, became the first National Historical Park. Architects restored the mansion in the 1930s and again in the 1960s to make it look as it did in the bitter winter of 1779–80, but the lack of documentation regarding the original house makes these restorations conjectural. The furnishings give a realistic picture of how Washington lived in the Ford mansion.

MOUNT VERNON

Mount Vernon, VA 22121
703-780-2000
www.mountvernon.org
NHL

From 1757 to1758, the hero of Valley Forge, George Washington, rebuilt and enlarged the Georgian house he inherited to bring it to the standards expected by the woman he married shortly thereafter—Martha Dandridge Custis, a young widow with two small children.

Washington saw little of his beloved Mount Vernon between 1775 and 1781. The plantation remained unscathed during the war, but the Washingtons lost some of their slaves, who fled to the British.

Originally built in 1743 by George Washington's half brother, Lawrence Washington, Mount Vernon was named for Lawrence Washington's commander in the British Navy, Edward Vernon.

George Washington remodeled and extended the formerly modest house of four rooms bisected by a central hall on each of two floors. He raised the roof and extended the house and outbuildings substantially. During the first fifteen years of his marriage, he lived there as a prosperous planter while serving in Virginia's House of Burgesses.

Washington's plans to enlarge Mount Vernon were interrupted by the American Revolution. Serving in the First and Second Continental Congresses, his fellow legislators appointed him commander in chief of the Continental Army in 1775. After the war, Washington added some final touches to Mount Vernon by building a large octagonal cupola at the center of the roof. That summer he went to Philadelphia to preside over the Constitutional Convention. Elected President in 1789, he was seldom at Mount Vernon until he retired after serving two terms as President, just two years before his death in 1799.

Like Thomas Jefferson's Monticello, Washington's Mount Vernon came close to being a national disaster instead of a national shrine. In 1858, fifty-nine years after Washington's death, the stately mansion on the banks of the Potomac was rapidly sinking. All but about 500 of the 8,000 acres comprising Washington's estate had long since been sold off by his heirs. The house itself was uninhabited, its furniture and furnishings gone, the outbuildings lying in ruins, the grounds neglected.

The owner of the property was John Augustine Washington, the first President's great-grandnephew. Unable to maintain the buildings and tired of the stream of visitors, John Washington had tried to sell the property to the Commonwealth of Virginia, but the state's legislators spurned the opportunity. He had refused private offers, perhaps mindful that Monticello had once fallen into private hands.

To the rescue came an obscure South Carolina invalid spinster, Ann Pamela Cunningham. "Let the women of America own and preserve Mt. Vernon," her mother wrote to her in 1853. With that as inspiration, she founded the Mount Vernon Ladies' Association, and five years later reached agreement with John Augustine Washington to purchase Mount Vernon for $200,000. Slowly Mount Vernon took shape as a historic house museum—only the second in the country—at an important moment when the country, drawn into an escalating sectional crisis, badly needed to rehabilitate Washington as a unifying symbol. Research in recent years—along with a willingness to be more candid about the founding fathers' involvement in slavery—has led to giving more attention to the slave quarters at Mount Vernon and the lives of their inhabitants.

GEORGE ROGERS CLARK MEMORIAL
401 South 2nd Street
Vincennes, IN 47591
812-882-1776
www.nps.gov/gero
NHL/NPS

In one of the epic feats of endurance and courage during the American Revolution, Lieutenant Colonel George Rogers Clark launched a daring assault deep in British-controlled territory in the Old Northwest. A tough, twenty-six-year-old frontiersman, Clark had orders to attack the three British settlements controlling the Illinois country—Vincennes on the Wabash River, Kaskaskia on the Mississippi, and Cahokia, near the confluence of the Missouri and Mississippi rivers. It seemed to many a suicidal mission, for how could several hundred frontiersmen vanquish an enemy five times as numerous (not to mention their Indian allies)? Yet with 175 men—which was far fewer than he had anticipated—Clark prevailed. Overcoming extraordinary obstacles, he captured the British at Fort Sackville near Vincennes in June 1778. In triumph, one of his officers wrapped the British flag around a rock and threw it into the Wabash River.

Like so many of the historic sites integral to the American Revolution, Fort Sackville was swallowed up by commercial and industrial development in the nineteenth century. In 1905, after more than a century, the Daughters of the American Revolution placed a stone marker on the approximate site of the fort. As the 150th anniversary of Clark's campaign approached in 1928, interest grew in further commemorating the extraordinary daring and strength of his frontiersmen-soldiers.

With city, county, state, and federal money, planning began for the George Rogers Memorial and National Historical Park. President Franklin D. Roosevelt dedicated the completed project on Flag Day, June 14, 1936. The George Rogers National Historical Park, situated along the Wabash River, approximately where the British Fort Sackville stood, was laid out in the 1930s. The round, granite memorial building, with a surrounding colonnade of sixteen granite Doric columns, is an example of Classical Revival planning. The memorial has thirty expansive granite steps leading to a monumental doorway surmounted by a carved eagle; inside is a bronze statue of George Rogers Clark.

COWPENS NATIONAL BATTLEFIELD

4001 Chesnee Highway
Chesnee, SC 29323
864-461-2828
www.nps.gov/cowp
NPS

On a frontier pasturing ground in South Carolina known as Cowpens, some of the men who had survived the Valley Forge encampment fought in a fierce and strategically important battle on January 16, 1781. Confronting Colonel Banastre Tarleton's Legion, the finest light corps in the British army, and a supporting artillery company, 830 Americans under the command of General Daniel Morgan were outmanned and outgunned but not outfought. In fact, they tore Tarleton's dreaded quick-strike legion apart. Of his 1,100 men, Tarleton saw 110 die and 530 surrender. It was a desperately needed American victory in the lower south, which had become the decisive theater in the last stage of the Revolutionary War.

In 1781, Cowpens was a grassy meadow speckled with tall hardwood trees—an "open wood . . . disadvantageous for the Americans and convenient for the British," as Tarleton described it. After the American Revolution, this crucial battlefield returned to its original use as a place to fatten cattle before sending them to market. Later, stripped of its woods, Southerners converted it to cotton cultivation. Not until 1929 did Cowpens begin to take shape as a national shrine. A monument to commemorate the battle was erected in 1932. Nearly 200 years after the battle, the Department of the Interior purchased 840 acres where they constructed trails, waysides, and a visitor center. In the late 1980s, a program began to restore the land to its appearance at the time of the battle. It will take another generation to complete the restoration of oak woods. Cowpens became a National Battlefield in 1929.

Marblehead Historic District

Marblehead, Mass.

The War at Sea

Marblehead, Massachusetts, is all about the sea—about tides and currents, boats and boat-building, fish and fishermen, wharves and buoys, the smell of shellfish and the sea. Located on a craggy peninsula separating Marblehead Harbor from Salem Harbor, the Marblehead Historic District embraces the center of the old Puritan town of Marblehead. In walking through the narrow, winding streets of the Historic District, half-a-mile square the visitor is never far from tidewater. The hillside town is built on a series of stony ledges, a place so rocky that visiting English evangelist George Whitefield wondered where the town buried its dead.

Taking in the salty sea smell of the mud flats at low tide, the traveler can wander among scores of wooden houses, shops, and churches that date to the eighteenth century. Boasting three stories, five bays, and double interior chimneys, the Georgian houses, including the stylish residences of merchants Jeremiah Lee, William Lee, and Robert "King" Hooper, still stand along Washington Street. The Lee house, built in 1768, is open to the public; visitors can view tasteful interior architecture, fine house furnishings, hand-painted scenic wallpaper, maritime artifacts, and eighteenth-century children's

Marblehead, an important shipbuilding center during the Revolution, became a backwater in the nineteenth century. Marblehead was industrialized far less than nearby coastal towns, which turned out to be an advantage from a preservationist point of view. Where shoe and textile factories changed the landscape in other towns only to be abandoned in the twentieth century, Marblehead retained much of its revolutionary-era maritime character.

furniture and toys. Nearby, studding Elm, Green, and Mugford Streets, are the more modest houses of sea captains, maritime artisans, and shopkeepers.

Lying at the north end of town is Fort Sewall, first built in 1644 on a rocky headland and enlarged in 1742 for defense against the French. The fort is a reminder of Marblehead's importance as a New England maritime stronghold. The powder house, erected in 1755 at the beginning of the French and Indian War, also recalls the town's strategic military importance. Today, Marblehead's Historic District has a greater concentration of buildings constructed before or during the American Revolution than any other New England town.

The Marblehead Historic District, established in 1984 and placed on the National Register of Historic Places, encompasses the nerve center of the town's pre-revolutionary fishing industry, its shipyards, and the focal point of its overseas commerce. Much of this commerce depended on fish. What tobacco was to Virginia, rice was to South Carolina, and wheat was to Pennsylvania, fish was to Massachusetts, and particularly to Marblehead, the colony's preeminent fishing port. Everywhere in town, fish were cured—on the beaches, in fields on the edge of town, and even in vacant town lots. Captain Francis Goelet, a merchant visiting from New York in 1750 found Marblehead "a dirty, irregular stinking place" where the stench of the fish polluted the air. But what affronted the New Yorker's nostrils meant only wealth to the salty Marbleheaders.

During the Revolution, Marblehead's reputation as a shipbuilding center grew. Its esteemed maritime workers—ship carpenters, sailmakers, anchor and chain forgers, rope spinners, riggers, and wood-carvers—crowded the Marblehead waterfront, which is now the main part of the Historic District. The first vessel that was taken into the Continental Navy was a schooner

Marblehead Historic District

Marblehead, MA 01945
781-631-2868

NRIS 84002402
NHL

SIGNIFICANCE
Since the 1630s, Marblehead, Massachusetts, has been intimately involved in the maritime history of New England as a center of fishing, boatbuilding, and coastal commerce. During the American Revolution, the seaport town contributed far beyond its population to the war at sea that helped secure American independence.

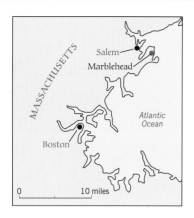

Along New England's rocky coast, fishing was a mainstay of the economy. Fish flakes—long, board tables—were used to dry cod before it was salted and packed into barrels for export.

built in Marblehead called *Hannah*. Other Marblehead schooners soon followed.

The American Revolution involved an intense naval war, but that conflict at sea was conducted mostly by the large fleets of the British, French, and Spanish. The Continental Congress and state leaders wanted to launch a deepwater American fleet, but they lacked the money to build more than a puny navy; and they had little experience in building large warships capable of taking on the British Navy. Nonetheless, a sea-minded people picked up victories here and there, slowed down the British if they could not defeat them, and—most of all—plagued the enemy's shipping with privateers that ranged the broad Atlantic in search of English prizes. That is how the men who lived in the Marblehead Historic District made their main contribution, although several hundred of them fought as bravely on land as their neighbors at sea.

The seafaring men of Marblehead fought in the Massachusetts state navy, in the Continental Navy, and in Colonel John Glover's "Webfoot Regiment," which rowed George Washington and his troops across the ice-clogged Delaware River to achieve a notable victory at Trenton on December 26, 1776. Glover's house, on King Street in the Historic District, is not as grand as the mansions of the wealthiest revolutionary-era merchants. But it was still a respectable house of the kind built by men on the move such as Glover, who had risen from shoemaker to ship owner and ship captain by the 1760s. Going through the front door, the visitor stands before a stairway leading to the second floor. Doors from the center hallway open into a parlor on one side, reserved for special occasions, and a sitting room on the other side, where Glover and his wife conducted business. Behind these rooms, fronting on what is now Glover Square, was a large kitchen. Upstairs, bedrooms with fireplaces accommodated Glover, his wife and their eleven children.

Most of the Marblehead men did not join Washington's army or the Massachusetts militia, but they rushed to enlist on the wooden hulled privateers. These hastily armed commercial ships bore "letters of marque and reprisal," which entitled them to prey on enemy shipping and bring to port any "prize" they captured that is, a vessel and its cargo—to be sold for the benefit of the

James Forten, Philadelphia's Boy Hero at Sea

When the British captured American pirate ships dogging the heels of their merchant ships, they held most of the American crews in prison ships, most of them anchored in New York City's Wallabout Bay. Many Marblehead privateers ended up on one of the most notorious of these death-trap ships, the *Old Jersey,* where thousands of captured Americans died. On the *Old Jersey* they would have met James Forten, an African-American teenager from Philadelphia whose experience at sea during the American Revolution became legendary.

According to family history, James Forten's great-grandfather had been brought in chains from Africa to the area around the Delaware River even before the English Quakers arrived in 1682, and his grandfather was one of the first Africans in Pennsylvania to purchase his freedom. Forten's father was a free black sail maker who died in 1776, seven years after James's birth. When he was old enough to read, James attended a school run by Quaker Anthony Benezet, where he learned to read and write. He also became influenced by the kindly Quaker's principles about the universality of humankind. Young James helped support his mother by working in Benezet's grocery store.

In 1781, the fifteen-year-old Forten signed on Stephen Decatur's twenty-two-gun pirate ship, the *Royal Louis,* as a powder boy. This launched a career filled with heroic acts that would gain him fame up and down the eastern seaboard. "Scarce wafted from his native shore, and perilled upon the dark blue sea,"

wrote William C. Nell, the country's first black historian, "than he found himself amid the roar of cannon, the smoke of blood, the dying, and the dead." In the bloody, but ultimately victorious engagement of the *Royal Louis* with the British ship *Lawrence,* Forten was the only survivor at his gun station.

Forten's colors showed even truer on the next voyage when his ship was captured by the British after a battle. The British captain's young son befriended Forten and offered free passage to England and the patronage of his family. "NO, NO!" Forten replied, according to Forten family legend, "I am here a prisoner for the liberties of my country; I never, NEVER, shall prove a traitor to her interests." His offer spurned, the British captain sent Forten to the *Old Jersey,* the rotting prison ship anchored in New York harbor. Released seven months later as the war was drawing to a close, the sixteen-year-old Forten made his way shoeless from New York to Trenton, New Jersey, and from there to Philadelphia.

As a deepwater sailor and veteran of the Revolution, it was natural that Forten would pursue his father's trade of sail making. In time, he became Philadelphia's most respected sail maker, operating a loft that employed a large crew of both black and white canvas workers. Forten would become a leader of the black community, an impassioned spokesman for their rights, a committed abolitionist who provided William Lloyd Garrison with the money to print his first issue of *The Liberator,* and the father of a large family of accomplished reformers.

Many more citizens signed up as privateers than as soldiers on the Continental warships. With official government sanctions, privateers could earn tremendous amounts of money by raiding British ships of their cargo.

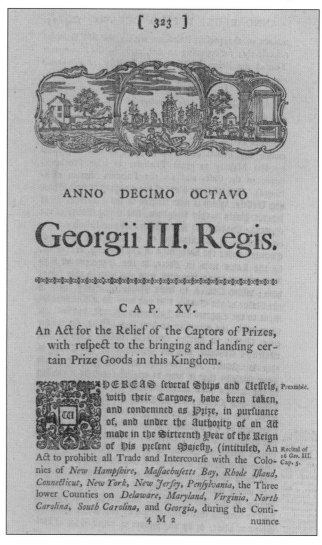

privateering crew. John Adams, representing Marblehead residents at the Continental Congress, called privateering "a short, easy, and infallible method of humbling the British."

Among nearly 1,000 privateers that sailed out of Massachusetts ports with state and Continental commissions, Marblehead shipowners figured prominently. Enticed by promises of great wealth—capturing a single unarmed English merchantman could reward a common seaman with a decade's wages—the American tars (sailors) were much more likely to sign on as privateers than answer to the patriotic notion of serving aboard a Continental warship. Indeed, ships of the Continental Navy often lay idle in port for want of a sufficient crew. Yet the privateers contributed to the patriot cause by diverting British warships that might otherwise have blockaded American ports and by seizing arms and supplies subsequently purchased by Washington's Continental Army and the state militias. Even Marblehead fishermen carried the war at sea to the British. Mounting swivel guns on their fishing smacks, they sailed in "wolf packs" to pick off any merchant vessel that lagged behind a British convoy.

American privateers captured 3,176 British merchantmen and privateers during the long war, but not without cost. Nothing indicates more fully how much Marblehead contributed to the war than the number of widows and orphans recorded in the 1780s. Today's visitor, walking through the Marblehead Historic District, can contemplate that in this town with about 650 houses and a total population of about 5,000 at the end of the Revolution, 459 widows and 865 orphans struggled to pick themselves up and find subsistence.

Commodore John Barry is shown with the accoutrements of a naval officer: his pistol sits on a drum, a sword rests against his right leg, and navigational mapsare on the table beside him.

Commemorating Their Own: The John Barry Monument

A bronze statue of John Barry, a naval hero of the American Revolution, stands at the center of Independence Square Park in Philadelphia. Barry was a man very large for his time—six feet, four inches—and his statue is even taller, measuring eight feet in height. Samuel Moore, a student of Philadelphia artist Thomas Eakins, sculpted the figure in 1907.

The Society of Friends of St. Patrick, an Irish mutual aid association founded in the eighteenth century, wanted to commemorate one of their own: the Catholic, Irish-born Barry, who had arrived in Philadelphia just before the outbreak of the Revolution. Schoolchildren learned little about Catholic and Irish contributions to the American nation because their textbooks were written primarily by Protestant historians with English roots and affections. Thus, 131 years after the Declaration of Independence, the Friends of St. Patrick commissioned a statue of Barry for the city of Philadelphia.

Even before the Declaration of Independence, Barry distinguished himself as the first American naval captain to capture a British warship. He also fought the last battles of the Continental Navy in American waters in late May 1781, off Sandy Hook, New Jersey, where he engaged and captured two English warships. He won his last battle, a month after hostilities had officially ended in March 1783, when he was carrying 100,000 Spanish-milled dollars to Philadelphia for the Continental treasury. Encountering two heavily gunned British frigates and a sloop, his gun crews outmatched the British. Poet Philip Freneau recorded that when the British challenged the *Alliance* to identify itself, Barry shouted out: "This is the United States ship *Alliance,* saucy Jack Barry, half Irishman, half Yankee. Who are you?"

Life in a British Prison Ship

The prison ship Old Jersey, *where the young James Forten spent seven months, was anchored in Wallabout Bay, where the Brooklyn Navy Yard now stands. A dismantled sixty-four-gun ship, it was a living hell for the thousands of prisoners packed into its below-deck compartments. Several eyewitness accounts of life on the prison ships paint a picture of what Forten endured. Ebenezer Fox, one of Forten's shipmates, wrote in his memoirs after the war of conditions aboard the* Old Jersey *in 1781.*

She was dismantled; her only spars were the bowsprit, a derrick that looked like a gallows, for hoisting supplies on board, and a flagstaff at the stern. The port-holes were closed and secured.... Each of us was permitted to retain whatever clothing and bedding we had brought ... and then we were directed to pass through a strong door on the starboard side,

The Old Jersey was a rotting hulk where disease, exposure to the elements, and terrible food decimated the captured Americans.

down a ladder leading to the main hatchway. I now found myself in a loathsome prison, among a collection of the most wretched and disgusting looking objects that I ever beheld in human form. Here was a motley crew, covered with rags and filth, visages pallid with disease, emaciated with hunger and anxiety, and retaining hardly a trace of their original appearance ... The *Jersey,* from her size and lying near the shore, was imbedded in the mud.... All the filth that accumulated among upwards of a thousand men was daily thrown overboard and would remain there till carried away by the tide. The impurity of the water may be easily conceived; and in this water our meat was boiled.... At sunset our ears were saluted with the insulting and hateful sound from our keepers, of "Down, rebels, down," and we were hurried below, the hatchways fastened over us and we were left to pass the night amid the accumulated horrors of sighs and groans, of foul vapor, a nauseous and putrid atmosphere, in a stifled and almost suffocating heat.... But little sleep ... could be enjoyed, ... for the vermin were so horribly abundant that all the personal cleanliness we could practise would not protect us from their attacks.

SALEM MARITIME NATIONAL HISTORIC SITE

174 Derby Street
Salem, MA 01970
978-740-1650
www.nps.gov/sama/
NPS

Like Marblehead, neighboring Salem played a key role in the maritime development of Massachusetts and a vital role in the war at sea during the American Revolution. Salem's waterfront has been altered far more than Marblehead's and has been converted to parkland and tourist attractions over the years since 1938, when the area was designated as a National Historic Site. Salem's decline in the late nineteenth century as a thriving shipping center led to the decay of the waterside warehouses, wharves, and maritime industries. But Salem's glory days in the age of sailing can still be recalled by walking along Derby Wharf (extended in 1806 to its present length), the bustling center of Elias Hasket Derby's commercial empire; the handsome Georgian brick house built by merchant Richard Derby in 1762 between Essex and Front Streets; First Church, erected in 1718; the wooden, gambel-roofed Crowninshield-Bentley House on Essex Street, built about 1727 by one of the town's preeminent mercantile families; and many other eighteenth-century buildings.

Salem's privateers were as active as Marblehead's sailors in disrupting British commerce during the American Revolution. Going to sea on the port's 158 privateering vessels, Salem sailors captured 458 British ships with a total tonnage greater than that claimed by any other American port. Salem suffered nonetheless through the disruption of the town's trade. The postwar revival led to the construction of handsome Federal-style houses on Chestnut Street, which is now a National Historic Landmark. The Peabody-Essex Museum, the oldest continuously functioning museum in the United States, is filled with exhibits that reflect Salem's maritime heritage in the colonial and revolutionary eras, as well as in the decades that followed.

JOHN PAUL JONES HOUSE

43 Middle Street
Portsmouth, NH 03801
603-436-8420
NHL

During his stay in Portsmouth, New Hampshire, in 1781–82, naval hero John Paul Jones lived as a boarder in a wooden oceanside house built in 1758. The house belonged to Mrs. Gregory Purcell, the widow of a merchant and ship captain who had died just three months after the Declaration of Independence was signed. A large house with two-and-a-half stories, two interior chimneys, and a gambrel roof, it served as a boardinghouse for many naval officers during the Revolutionary War. Although altered by the addition of a two-story frame wing in the early nineteenth century, the house exists today much as it did two centuries ago. The Portsmouth Historical Society, which acquired the building in 1919, uses it as its headquarters and displays it as a historical house of the revolutionary period.

At the outset of the American Revolution, nobody would have guessed that an out-of-work, poor, twenty-eight-year-old immigrant who had barely escaped murder charges would become one of the new nation's naval heroes. Born John Paul in Kirkbean, Scotland, he went

When John Paul Jones lived in this house in Portsmouth, New Hampshire, he supervised the construction of the America, *the first and only seventy-four-gun ship built for the Continental Navy.*

to sea at age twelve, where he served on several slave ships. In 1773, facing charges of flogging a ship's carpenter to death, Paul fled to Virginia, where he added Jones to his name to help conceal his identity. The Continental Congress appointed him to fit out the first naval ship it procured and appointed him a lieutenant in December 1775. Thus began a career of sea exploits that made Jones a hero by the end of the war. He was celebrated for the capture of sixteen British ships early in the conflict and his hit-and-run attacks in 1778 on England's western coast. His most celebrated victory, however, occurred the next year, aboard the *Bonhomme Richard,* a converted old clumsy, unresponsive, and lightly gunned East Indiaman, where he and his crew defeated the British warship *Serapis.* It was during this battle that he made his famous declaration, "I have not yet begun to fight."

Ten years after John Paul Jones waged his three-hour fight under a full moon against the Serapis, *an English naval officer, William Elliott, painted this view of the struggle.*

VALCOUR BAY

Plattsburgh, NY 12901
NHL

The rocky, wooded Valcour Island, about two miles long and a bit more than one mile wide, rises off the west shore of Lake Champlain about four miles south of Plattsburgh, New York. Valcour Bay, also known as Valcour Sound, between the island and the west shore of the lake, is about three-quarters of a mile wide. New York's Clinton State Forest occupies much of the island. Today it is a place to hike, swim, picnic, and boat; but 225 years ago, the water ran red with blood and the air was filled with cannon and musket fire.

Valcour Island, all but forgotten in the history books, was the scene of a critical rearguard American action. The naval engagement in October 1776 on Valcour Bay was the opening thrust of the British invasion of northern New York. General Guy Carleton knew that establishing British control of the Hudson River–Lake Champlain waterways in that area was crucial to severing the New England colonies from the mid-Atlantic colonies.

When Carleton's fleet of twenty-nine vessels arrived on October 11, 1776, a seven-hour battle began. The Americans were badly outgunned and severely harassed by several hundred Iroquois warriors who raked them with musket fire from both the mainland and Valcour Island. Arnold's force fought bravely but lost almost all its ships and several hundred men. Yet by inflicting damage on Carleton's fleet, the Americans convinced him that he could not make good his losses in time to capture Fort Ticonderoga on Lake Champlain until the next season. Carleton's withdrawal of his army to Canada allowed the Americans to regroup and build their strength during the winter and spring so that they were able to defeat the British at Saratoga in October 1777—a turning point in the Revolution.

Faneuil Hall

Boston, Mass.

Revolutionary Reform

Modern Boston has been built around Faneuil Hall, leaving it as a sole reminder of the eighteenth century. Today, Faneuil Hall's swarms of visitors, many of them American, European, and Asian tourists, receive only faint echoes of the building's venerable past and historical significance.

C an America be happy under a government of her own?" wrote Thomas Paine in answer to an attack on his *Common Sense,* the pamphlet published in January 1776 that galvanized the Americans to declare their independence. "As happy as she please; she hath a blank sheet to write upon." In these two pithy sentences, Paine captured the little-noticed side of the American Revolution—the struggle of the patriots, after they cast themselves into a state of nature by renouncing the English charters and laws under which they had functioned, to begin remaking their society and their country. What kind of laws, political arrangements, and constitutionally protected liberties did they wish to live under? By what means should they create new state governments? Would everyone enjoy the inalienable rights expressed in the Declaration of Independence? If the slate had been wiped clean, who was entitled to put new words on the slate and how would people with different agendas for the future resolve their differences? These questions, faced in each

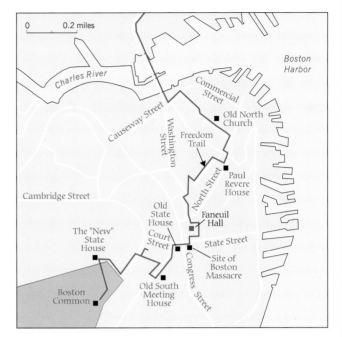

of the thirteen new states, brought forth a torrent of reformist ideas. Some would be implemented, others defeated, and others deferred. Among the sites of reformist ideas, Boston's Faneuil Hall was one of the most important.

Boston's Faneuil Hall was a vital and vibrant site of debate and decision making during and long after the revolutionary era because it was here that Bostonians assembled for their beloved town meetings. Here they elected sheriffs, constables, and other local officers, chose delegates to the Massachusetts House of Representatives, decided how much to pay schoolteachers or whether widows should receive firewood, and debated the issues of the day. As events led to the American Revolution, Faneuil Hall became a critically important place of assembly and a venue for celebrating revolutionary victories and planning for the future.

With a gift of money in 1740 from the successful French Huguenot immigrant Peter Faneuil, Bostonians built Faneuil Hall with the first floor designed to serve as a public market and the second floor to host public meetings. Designed by John Smibert, Boston's finest portrait painter at the time, and called a "Hall of LIBERTY" by Boston's *Weekly Magazine,* Faneuil Hall immediately became a center of impassioned arguing, petition-signing, and noisy gatherings after its opening in 1742. Even its construction was controversial because nearly half of

Bostonians voted against accepting Faneuil's gift because they believed that this public market would not serve the ordinary consumer well. At the dedication of the building, while praising Faneuil's generosity, James Lovell, Master of the Boston Latin School, prayed, "May Liberty always spread its joyful wings over this place. May Loyalty to a king under whom we enjoy that Liberty ever remain our character." Lovell, who became a Tory during the Revolution, saw only the first half of his wish fulfilled.

Fire destroyed the interior of Faneuil Hall in 1761, but it was rebuilt two years later in the face of stiff opposition from those who had always opposed a public market. Its red-brick Georgian exterior, with nine tall arched windows on each floor of its 100-foot length, is surmounted by a graceful tower topped with a gilded grasshopper weathervane. Now it would emerge as "the cradle of liberty," so called because the fiery lawyer and pamphleteer James Otis, Jr., dedicated the rebuilt hall in March 1763 to the cause of liberty. Thomas Young, a Tea Party participant and one of the Revolution's most avid reformers (first in Albany and Boston, then in Newport and Philadelphia) called Faneuil Hall

> a noble school where the meanest citizen . . . may deliver his sentiments and give his suffrage in very important matters, as freely as the greatest Lord in the Land! Here men may be trained up for the Senate, for the field, for any department in the state where manly prudence and address are required.

The question of who would be allowed to vote and hold office would be one of the pivotal issues of the revolutionary era. Reformers such as Young believed that the right to vote should be extended to all free adult white males, and some were even ready to extend it to women. Young thanked "my Creator" for making him a Bostonian because in this city "a haughty coxcomb wou'd be despised, a tyrant abhorred among them. . . . We abound with middling men! Our greatest personages are not above a laudable concern for the welfare of the meanest . . . . Many common tradesmen in this town display the wisdom and eloquence of Athenian Senators." A later historian of Boston, Samuel Adams Drake, called Faneuil Hall "the centre from which the voice of the people of Boston should proceed."

Faneuil Hall

Dock Square
Boston, MA 02109
617-242-5675
www.nps.gov/bost

NRIS 66000368
NHL/NPS

DATE BUILT
1740–42; rebuilt 1763

ARCHITECT
John Smibert

SIGNIFICANCE
Originally a public market, Faneuil Hall also was the scene of speeches, debate, and decision making as Boston reformers led the citizenry to independence. For many decades thereafter, the hall continued to echo with speeches as Bostonians decided on the form of government they wished to live under and how they would follow the principles set forth in the Declaration of Independence.

Thomas Young might well have had Samuel Adams in mind when he spoke of the eloquence of "common tradesmen." A cousin of John Adams, Samuel was a brewer whose talents developed as an orator rather than as a businessman. The public meeting room on the second floor of Faneuil Hall became his main stage. He not only emerged as the leader of the radical, pro-independence party in Boston but he became a defender of the common people. For Jefferson, he was "truly the *Man of the Revolution*." For John Adams, he was "born and tempered a wedge of steel to split the knot of *lignum vitae* [literally, 'wood of life']" that tied the colonies to England. To the royal governor of Massachusetts, Thomas Hutchinson, he was the greatest firebrand "in the King's dominion." Some said he "taught his dog Queue to bite every Red Coat he saw," and it is sure that he took John Adams's young son by hand to the Boston Commons to teach him to hate British soldiers.

In Faneuil Hall, Sam Adams was at his best. Heartily believing that the people were not "sheeplike masses" or "an unthinking herd," as many of his contemporaries claimed, he roused the citizens in campaigns to stop the importation and use of British goods, appealed to them to resist British policies, and reminded them repeatedly that "they can judge, as well as their betters, when there is a danger of *slavery*." It was also in Faneuil Hall that Adams denounced the Sugar Act of 1764 (which imposed a tax on Bostonians and a restriction on their trade) and drafted a statement urging its repeal.

It was in Faneuil Hall that Bostonians gathered one day after the Boston Massacre in 1770 to hear Adams's rousing speech advocating the immediate withdrawal of British troops. It was here that a whole crowd gathered to deal with the Tea Act crisis in 1773—only to adjourn to Old South Church since Faneuil Hall's capacity of 1,200 was too small to contain the outpouring of

John Singleton Copley painted Samuel Adams in a simple wool suit with no embroidery and a partially unbuttoned waistcoat, all suggesting the patriot leader's disdain for "proper" appearances. His Boston neighbors outfitted him before sending him as their delegate to the Continental Congress, lest his threadbare clothes embarrass Massachusetts.

townspeople. A year later, after the Parliamentary "Coercive Acts" closed the port of Boston in an attempt to strangle the town into compliance with British policy, Adams moderated the town meeting at Faneuil Hall to consider what to do in this emergency. Within a few months, those thrown out of work by the port's closure went to Faneuil Hall to explain their circumstances to a relief committee for the poor and receive aid payments.

Adams also meant to reform the emerging nation by restoring the public virtue he believed was slipping away. A strict Puritan, he urged temperance, frugality, the banning of theater in Boston, and above all else, the sacrifice of private advantage for the good of the community. Part of his appeal in Boston as the Revolution approached was his fervid criticism of the aristocratic flaunting of wealth by Governor Hutchinson and his clique—men who indulged themselves with elaborate weddings, ornately furnished mansions, and grandiose portraits. His creed was moral reform. At the Continental Congress in Philadelphia in 1775, he opposed a festive ball in honor of Martha Washington and had it canceled as inappropriate to these "melancholy times." Opposed to luxury and extravagance, he took pride in his modest means. "I glory in being what the world calls a poor man," he wrote his wife.

Adams's reformist zeal also extended to the social arrangements of the sexes. He leaned toward gender equality, especially in marriage, where he thought men "govern too much." A democratic partnership would serve both the family and the nation better, he argued. He also believed Boston should do more to improve the education of girls.

For the British occupying Boston, the "cradle of liberty" at Faneuil Hall was hardly popular. On the Sunday following the battles at Lexington and Concord, Boston citizens came to Faneuil Hall to work out an agreement with British General Thomas Gage about leaving town. It was a bitter business. Many men who had fought in the Seven Years War were forced to surrender their arms to Gage before leaving, which they found humiliating. Later, in 1775–76, the British quartered their troops on the first floor of Faneuil Hall and used the second floor as a theater rather than as the town meeting venue. Those who maintained their allegiance to the British—known as loyalists or Tories—remained in the city,

This political cartoon shows Boston's abolitionist leader William Lloyd Garrison trying to protect his Scottish abolitionist friend George Thompson from a Boston mob after he spoke in Faneuil Hall.

sometimes attending dramas in Faneuil Hall that ridiculed the patriots.

Faneuil Hall was enlarged in 1805–06, as well it might since the revolutionary town of 15,000 had swelled to a city of 30,000. The celebrated architect Charles Bulfinch doubled its width, originally forty feet, added a third story, relocated the cupola, and made it more elegant. When it opened, people flocked to see Gilbert Stuart's huge painting of George Washington's victory at Dorchester Heights in 1776. Faneuil Hall was further embellished in 1818 with John Trumbull's gigantic eighteen-foot-wide painting of the Declaration of Independence being presented to the Continental Congress. Four years later, when Boston replaced its town meetings with a municipal government with a mayor and aldermen, Faneuil Hall lost its primacy as the venue of popular politics and urban democracy.

However, Faneuil Hall remained a site for patriotic celebrations. By the 1820s, Bostonians were celebrating the Fourth of July with massive processions, and when the Marquis of Lafayette arrived on his grand American tour in 1824, he toasted: "May Faneuil Hall ever stand a monument to teach the world that resistance to oppression is a duty." In 1835, 800 workingmen feasted at Faneuil Hall after parading through the streets—the first time they had held their own July Fourth celebrations by themselves. A few months later, from the other end of the political spectrum, upper-class Bostonians assembled in the hall to condemn Boston's antislavery society as "a *revolutionary society*," as a handbill produced by Boston editor James Homer termed it, and to offer a purse of $100 to the first person who brought the touring Scottish abolitionist George Thompson "[to] the tar kettle."

For the remainder of the nineteenth century, Bostonians regarded Faneuil Hall as a special place for commemorative and political events, and invariably orators invoked its importance in the revolutionary era. For example, abolitionist leaders denounced the Mexican War of 1848 in Faneuil Hall. In 1873 the Woman's Suffrage Association strung a banner inscribed "Taxation Without Representation is Tyranny" across the stage from which some of the century's most famous orators—Wendell Phillips, Frederick Douglass, Lucy Stone, and William Lloyd Garrison—exhorted a packed hall. "If Sam Adams could speak today," thundered Phillips, "[he would] stand exactly where he did in his age—at the very head of the van of the reformers of his age," in favor of enfranchising women and arm-in-arm with those trying "to prevent money from accumulating in the aristocratic class."

After more than a century of standing as a place for reformers to hold their banners aloft, Faneuil Hall decayed as Boston's waterfront became blighted like so many others along the eastern seaboard. Then it reemerged, though put to very different uses. In 1974, the U.S. Congress and the National Park Service created Boston National Historical Park, which links sixteen historical sites along a two-and-a-half-mile Freedom Trail. The trail included Faneuil Hall and several other sites, such as Old South Meeting House, the Old State House, the Boston Massacre Site, the Paul Revere House, and Old North Church. Then, in 1976, urban developers recycled the venerable but badly decayed Faneuil Hall, along with Quincy Market, in order to initiate a major facelift of the Boston waterfront area. Transforming Faneuil Hall into a maze of upscale shops, restaurants, and food stalls, the developers capitalized on the building's waterfront ambience and created a major tourist attraction. A sculpture of Sam Adams by Anne Whitney stands guard behind the building.

PENNSYLVANIA HOSPITAL

Pine Street between Eighth and Ninth Streets
Philadelphia, PA 19107
215-829-8796
www.pahosp.com
NHL

Revolutionary fervor spread through all thirteen colonies because reform-minded revolutionists appeared in every town and city. In Philadelphia, a young doctor named Benjamin Rush personified the notion, sometimes verging on dreams of a new millennium, that American society could be perfected while its people gained independence. This spirit of reform in Philadelphia, North America's largest city at the time, was brilliantly represented in brick and mortar in the Pennsylvania Hospital for the Sick Poor.

The Pennsylvania Hospital for the Sick Poor, where Rush practiced for many years, is the oldest public building in Philadelphia except for Independence Hall, and it is the city's oldest

Pennsylvania Hospital's Georgian-style exterior looks much as it did during the Revolution. In a pioneering effort to use the concept of matching funds to raise money for the construction of public buildings, the Pennsylvania Assembly, urged on by Benjamin Franklin, provided £2,000—about $200,000 today—on the condition that private individuals raise an equal amount.

reform institution still in existence. It began to take form in 1751, twenty-five years before the Declaration of Independence, when Dr. Thomas Bond, the city's leading physician, promoted the idea of a hospital where injured and sick workingmen in Philadelphia could regain their health.

Promoted vigorously by Benjamin Franklin, the hospital attracted public funds as well as private donations. The east wing of the building opened its doors in 1756 with three physicians pledging to serve there for three years without pay. Rush, as civic-minded as Benjamin Franklin, was appointed as a staff physician in 1783. The seal of the institution shows the good Samaritan caring for the sick man with the inscription, "Take care of him, and I will repay thee."

The east wing served the city well for more than three decades, but Philadelphia's swelling population required the hospital to expand. A west wing was completed in 1796, and the center building connecting the two wings was finished in 1802. A skylight over the main building provided light for an amphitheater where operations were performed until 1863 in front of young student doctors. Situated between Eighth and Ninth Streets and between Spruce and Pine, the east wing contained wards for men on the first floor, wards for women on the second

floor, cells for the mentally ill in the basement, and rooms in the attic for isolation cases.

The exterior of the brick, Georgian-style hospital remains largely unchanged today, as does the handsome stairway in the main building. The restored amphitheater and museum exhibits tell visitors something of the eighteenth-century medical practice of men such as Bond and Rush. The hospital grounds contain a recreated eighteenth-century herb garden.

While serving as a young doctor in Philadelphia on the eve of the Revolution, three reforms came to dominate Rush's thinking: abolishing slavery; establishing public education, including the education of women; and encouraging temperance. Even before the Paris Peace Treaty of 1783 officially ended the war, Rush was engaged in a series of reforms that added up to a program for remaking the nation. He stepped up his attacks on slavery. Returning to the topic of female education, which he had promoted as early as 1770, he penned a pamphlet in 1787 called "Thoughts upon Female Education," which put him in the forefront of those who believed that the salvation of the new United States depended on an educated population of women. This paralleled his "Plan for Establishing Public Schools in Pennsylvania," a visionary program for state-supported schools that would lift the poor and laboring classes into a position where they could compete with the well-to-do for whatever opportunities presented themselves.

Atop this system of free public schools, Pennsylvania would erect a state university in Philadelphia and feeder colleges in other parts of the state. It would take many years beyond Rush's death in 1813 to establish this system, but he provided the theoretical basis for it: "Every member of the community is interested in the propagation of virtue and knowledge in the state." When Rush died in 1813, the nation lost the premier reformer of the Revolutionary era. Upon hearing of his death, John Adams wrote to Thomas Jefferson: "I know of no character, living or dead, who has done more real good in America."

LIBRARY HALL
105 South Fifth Street
Philadelphia, PA 19106
215-440-3400
NHL

The Library Company of Philadelphia's Library Hall, another site of American reform, was conceived before the Revolution; but the years of tumult delayed its construction until 1789–90. Built on Fifth Street across from Independence Hall, its Georgian facade fitted in comfortably with its larger neighbor. The building was demolished in 1884, but the American Philosophical Society built a larger version of it in 1959.

As was the case for many important buildings of the revolutionary era, the competition for the design of Library Hall was won by an amateur architect, an English immigrant doctor named William Thornton. The two-story brick building, with four white pilasters and generous windows, was approached by a curving double flight of marble steps that led to an arched doorway. Above the doorway was a marble pedestal on which stood a life-size sculpture of Benjamin Franklin. The facade of Library Hall today is faithful to all the main architectural features of the original building

If Philadelphia was known as the center of the American Enlightenment, the American Philosophical Society and the Library Company of Philadelphia were the nerve centers of the city's reform-minded citizens. Both the Philosophical Society and the Library Company owed much to Benjamin Franklin, arguably the most fertile organizer of urban reform in his era. In 1731, still in his twenties, Franklin assembled a group of his artisan friends to found the Library Company of Philadelphia. And twelve years later, he founded what would become the American Philosophical Society in 1769. Library Hall became the gathering point for men devoted to exploring useful knowledge. It also became a place for disseminating their ideas for perfecting human society on both sides of the Atlantic.

Peyton Randolph House

Williamsburg, Va.

The African Americans' Revolution

A ll through the spring of 1775, the twenty-seven slaves toiling in Peyton Randolph's stately dwelling in Williamsburg, Virginia, pondered startling new developments that promised to affect their lives. Their master was one of Virginia's most important figures; he was speaker of Virginia's legislative body that met in Williamsburg, vestryman of Bruton Parish Anglican church, and Virginia delegate to the Continental Congress meeting in Philadelphia. All of Williamsburg had heard that the colony's royal governor, Lord Dunmore, threatened to declare freedom to any slaves in retaliation for what he regarded as Virginia's treasonous opposition to British policies.

Whether in the enormous kitchen-quarter behind the Randolph house or in their adjacent quarters, the slaves must have calculated their next move. Then the kitchen buzzed with news in early November 1775 that their master had died suddenly of a stroke in Philadelphia. Nearly simultaneously, on November 5, they learned that Lord Dunmore, a figure every slave knew by sight, did what he had previously threatened: He issued a proclamation that promised "freedom to any slaves who desert rebellious masters and who serve in the king's forces." Eight of these enslaved Africans—Aggy, Billy, Eve, Sam, Lucy, George, Henry, and Peter—seized the moment. Slipping away from Randolph's house, probably at night, they eluded the slave patrols that walked Williamsburg's streets and reached the British forces not far from town.

The African Americans who prepared meals in the

Enslaved Africans did much of the work involved in constructing the Randolph house, including firing bricks, cutting boards, glazing windows, and blacksmithing ironwork.

kitchen-quarter and toiled in the Randolph house were among the thousands who had to make decisions during the course of a long and tumultuous war. Their labor in the mansion was, to be sure, not as hard and exhausting as that of the thirty-six enslaved field hands on Randolph's two plantations in James City County. These domestic slaves prepared the food, cleaned the thirteen richly furnished rooms of the Randolph mansion, tended the gardens, spun thread and wove cloth, curried and shoed the horses, mended harnesses, loaded and unloaded wagons, did the carpentry and blacksmithing, waited tables, and attended to scores of other household jobs. But for most of them, slavery was as galling and their freedom as precious as it was for plantation slaves.

The Randolph house was erected in three stages between 1715 and 1725. It was one of Williamsburg's largest dwellings, befitting the status of Peyton Randolph's father, Sir John Randolph, who was Speaker of the House of Burgesses and an eminent attorney. Growing up in this house, Peyton Randolph followed his father into law and became Speaker of the House of Burgesses in 1766. In 1774 he presided over the First Continental Congress in Philadelphia, and a year later he served briefly as president of the Second Continental Congress. Meanwhile his slave holdings grew. The house symbolizes the paradox of the Americans fighting for independence and liberty while holding one-fifth of the population in lifelong bondage.

The dawn of liberty for Africans in Virginia began in Williamsburg, the colony's capital. The growing rift between England and its colonies had set slaves to thinking about their own yearning for freedom. Even as battles broke out at Concord and Lexington in April 1775, several groups of slaves in Tidewater, Virginia, assembled to plan rebellions, and soon they began to look at Virginia's royal governor for encouragement. From that point on, black Virginians began to associate their quest for freedom with the prospect that the British would do what their colonial patriot masters would not: declare them free. That exhilarating idea seemed within reach in November 1775, when Governor Dunmore issued his memorable proclamation.

The twenty-seven slaves associated with the Peyton Randolph House, as well as the thirty-six who labored on Randolph's nearby plantations, faced circumstances

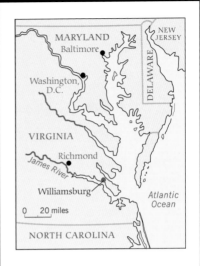

Peyton Randolph, a cousin of Thomas Jefferson, took his slave John Harris with him to Philadelphia in 1775. After he died suddenly on October 23, 1775, Randolph was buried at Christ's Church in Philadelphia. Harris ran away from Randolph's nephew, Edmund Randolph, to whom he had been bequeathed, in December 1777.

Peyton Randolph House

Colonial Williamsburg
Williamsburg, VA 23081
800-447-8679
www.history.org

NRIS 70000863
NHL

DATE BUILT
1717

ORIGINAL OWNER
William Robertson

SIGNIFICANCE
The Peyton Randolph house in
Virginia's capital was a site of
American revolutionary fervor
because Randolph was a leading
Virginia delegate to the
Continental Congress. From
this house, at least eight of
Randolph's many slaves fled
to gain their freedom.

and challenges that confronted nearly half a million
enslaved Africans in America, almost 200,000 of them
in Virginia. Like so many enslaved Africans in other
parts of the colonies, Randolph's slaves probably cared
little about the revenue stamps and tea parties that
brought their master to the forefront of intercolonial politics. However, they were profoundly aroused by the
white colonists' language and modes of protest against
the British revenue policies.

The African workers' yearning for freedom was as
old as their presence in the colonies, but by the early
1770s they began to see new opportunities for securing
their freedom amid the disruptions of the larger society
in rebellion. The response of enslaved Africans to the
Revolution hinged primarily on achieving freedom; if the
British provided most of the opportunities for freedom,
then it was logical that when they had the freedom to
choose, most joined the British ranks.

By its very nature, the Revolutionary War created
completely new situations for slaves. With the massive
movement of both civilian and military populations
through nearly every major seaport from Savannah to
Boston, urban slaves had unprecedented chances for
making their personal declarations of independence and
for destabilizing the institution of slavery. Likewise, as
Tory and Patriot militia units crisscrossed the countryside and plundered the property of their enemies, slaves
found ways of tearing gaping holes in the fabric of slavery. Many were women, including Eve, who probably
served as the personal servant of Peyton Randolph's
wife. Others were slaves who received the most favorable treatment and were thought by their masters and
mistresses to be immune from the itch for freedom.
Such was Johnny, or John Harris as he called himself.
Randolph had taken Harris, his mulatto personal servant, to Philadelphia on several occasions to serve him
while he attended the sessions of the Continental
Congress. But after Randolph's death in late 1775, Harris
found himself, by the provision of his master's will, the
property of Edmund Randolph, his master's nephew.
Two years later, Harris escaped from Edmund Randolph
to live as a freeman.

Largely built by slave labor, the gabled, two-story
Randolph house with a large central chimney remained
only briefly in the Randolph family after its owner's death.

When his widow died eight years later, in 1783, the house passed into other hands. For more than a century and a half, it underwent additions and alterations, but its interior yellow pine paneling mostly remained, testifying to the craftsmanship of Williamsburg's carpenters.

The house was acquired by the Colonial Williamsburg Foundation in 1938, one of eighty-two surviving eighteenth-century buildings in what had been Virginia's capital during the colonial and revolutionary decades. The Randolph house was restored several years later and was opened to the public in 1968. Using an inventory of the house's furnishings in 1776, Colonial Williamsburg did more extensive work from 1996 to 2001 that restored the house faithfully to its Revolutionary War character and reconstructed added outbuildings. After detailed archaeological investigation, this restoration included the rebuilding of the massive detached kitchen with its covered brick walkway to the main house so often trod upon by Randolph's slaves.

For many years, the presentation of the restored Randolph house to millions of admiring visitors to Colonial Williamsburg included little reference to the colonial owner's slaves or the flight of eight of them to the British during the Revolution. This was because John D. Rockefeller's huge investment in recreating colonial Williamsburg nearly obliterated memory of the fact that nearly half of Williamsburg's population in the late

Prince Whipple, a free black from Portsmouth, New Hampshire, holds the stroke oar in Emanuel Leutze's painting of George Washington's Christmas-night crossing of the ice-choked Delaware River. Three years later, Whipple was one of twenty "Natives of Africa" who petitioned the New Hampshire legislature unsuccessfully to free all slaves.

eighteenth century was African American. But the "pickled past" at Colonial Williamsburg, as the architectural critic Ada Louise Huxtable called it, began to change in the 1970s, shortly after the restoration of the Peyton Randolph house. Today, Colonial Williamsburg is one of the nation's premier interpretive historical sites. At the Randolph house, programs on "Enslaving Virginia" frankly present the realities of slavery during the era of the American Revolution. The slaves who toiled at the Randolph house have been restored to memory, and the Randolph house now is a site for exploring race relations while contemplating architectural and decorative history.

Although far more enslaved Africans served with the British than with the patriots for the simple reason that the war where the best chance for freedom lay, thousands of African Americans, most of them free, served with state militia and navy units and in the Continental Army

Black Americans Insist on Their Unalienable Rights

 With the rhetoric of unalienable rights fueling the colonial protests against new English policies, enslaved Africans in New England and other parts of the continent began applying the colonists' logic about natural rights to their own depraved condition. Almost a year before the battles at Lexington and Concord, "a great number of blacks of the Province . . . held in a state of slavery within a free and Christian country," as their petition phrased it, implored the Massachusetts legislature to square its actions with its rhetoric. The Massachusetts legislature made no response to four petitions of this kind, but sentiment grew that slavery affronted revolutionary principles.

Your petitioners apprehend we have in common with all other men a natural right to our freedoms without being depriv'd of them by our fellow men as we are a freeborn people and have never forfeited this blessing by any compact or agreement whatever. But we were unjustly dragged by the cruel hand of power from our dearest friends and some of us stolen from the bosoms of our tender parents and from a populous pleasant and plentiful country and brought hither to be made slaves for life in a Christian land. Thus we are deprived of everything that hath a tendency to make life even tolerable. . . . If there had been any law to hold us in bondage. . . . there never was any to enslave our children for life when born in a free country. We therefore beg your Excellency and Honours will . . . cause an act of the legislative to be passed that we may obtain our natural right, our freedoms, and our children to be set at liberty at the year of twenty one.

Crispus Attucks, the First Martyr of the American Revolution, King (now State) Street, Boston, March 5th, 1770. Page 16.

and Navy. At first, white leaders were unwilling to put blacks in the armed forces, whether slave or free. But driven by manpower shortages, the states in 1777 began to accept free blacks in militia units while recruiting sergeants quietly accepted slaves in place of their masters, often with private agreements that the slave, if he survived the war, would earn his freedom. This occurred in the South as well as the North. Some of Peyton Randolph's neighbors in Williamsburg rented slaves to the navy and army as ship pilots, wagoners, and common laborers. This process was repeated in many other locales.

By publishing The Colored Patriots of the American Revolution in 1855, the Boston historian William Nell became the first African American to draw attention to the sacrifices made by blacks during the American Revolution. Fighting to end slavery, Nell chose not to mention that many slaves joined with the British to secure their freedom.

Phillis Wheatley: America's Revolutionary Black Poet

 Few who encountered the frail young girl in Boston as the Revolution approached doubted that she was touched with genius. She arrived almost naked at about age seven on a slave ship and was sold at auction. Named Phillis Wheatley by her owners, within sixteen months she had "attained the English language . . . to such a degree as to read any, the most difficult parts of the Sacred Writings," according to her master. At age fourteen she was writing lucid poetry. At sixteen she wrote her first patriot poem chastising British customs officer who murdered a teenager protesting the British soldiers who occupied Boston in 1768. The young black woman was not a radical; however, by 1772 she was weaving a muffled plea for an end to slavery into her odes to American rights and American resistance to British policies. In a poem addressed to the English Secretary of State for the American colonies, Wheatley bared her sorrow and pain about enslavement.

Phillis Wheatley's likeness, used as the frontispiece of a volume of her poems, is by the black Boston artist Scipio Moorhead, Wheatley's friend and a poet himself.

Should you, my lord, while you peruse my song,
Wonder from whence my love of Freedom sprung,
Whence flow these wishes for the common good,
By feeling hearts alone best understood,
I young in life, by seeming cruel fate
Was snatch'd from Afric's fancy'd happy seat:
What pangs excruciating must molest,
What sorrows labour in my parent's breast?
Steel'd was that soul and by no misery mov'd
That from a father seiz'd his babe belov'd:
Such, such my case. And can I then but pray
Others may never feel tyrannic sway?

LEMUEL HAYNES HOUSE

Route 149
South Granville, NY 12832
NHL

Born in 1753 of an enslaved African and a white woman, Lemuel Haynes was indentured as an infant to a minister in the frontier town of Granville, Massachusetts. The day after the skirmishes between British troops and colonial patriots at Lexington and Concord, Haynes enlisted as a minuteman. Marching with his militia company, he participated in the siege of Boston in 1775. Soon he fought with Ethan Allen's Green Mountain Boys at Fort Ticonderoga, on the shore of Lake Champlain, where the Americans took the fort from the British. In 1776 he joined the Continental Army and saw action in many battles.

Haynes lived in many places before his final residence. Haynes' house, a basic two-story New England frame structure with a floor made of wide peg-laid boards, was built in 1793. A large fireplace with Dutch oven heated the home. Haynes purchased the house in 1822 and lived in it until his death eleven years later. The house, on a two-acre plot, descended to the family of Lemuel Haynes, Jr., and was historically restored in 1967.

After the American Revolution, Haynes supported himself doing farm labor while preparing for a lifetime in the ministry. Licensed to preach in 1780—the first ordination of a black clergyman in the United States—he led a white congregation in Middle Granville, Massachusetts. There he met Elizabeth Babbitt, a white woman who bucked the tide against interracial marriage. Their marriage lasted for more than fifty years and produced ten children. In 1788, Haynes became the pastor in Rutland, Vermont, where he served for thirty years. After a long tenure there, Haynes moved on to his final pastorate in South Granville, New York, where he served through his seventies. After Haynes died, his biographer, Timothy Matthew Cooley, called him "a sanctified genius," a man whose life story could "hardly fail to mitigate the unreasonable prejudices against the Africans in our land."

MOTHER BETHEL AFRICAN METHODIST EPISCOPAL CHURCH

419 South Sixth Street
Philadelphia, PA 19147
215-925-0616
NHL

Richard Allen, a black founding father, purchased a plot of land at Sixth and Lombard

A wooden blacksmith's shop set on wheels and hauled by horses for several blocks served as the first church ministered by Richard Allen in Philadelphia. The church was fondly called "Mother Bethel."

Streets in 1794 and seven weeks later was holding services in a converted blacksmith's shop hauled to this site. This plot is the oldest real estate in the country continuously owned by African Americans, and Allen's church was one of the first free black churches established in the United States.

Allen played a part in the American Revolution. Purchasing his freedom in 1780, he hauled salt from Rehoboth, Maryland, for the American army while preaching the Methodist message. In 1786, three years after the war ended, Allen arrived in Philadelphia at the request of white Methodists to preach to the growing community of free blacks. He coestablished the Free African Society, the first free black organization in the mid-Atlantic region, just weeks before the Constitutional Convention met in the city. Black Philadelphians flocked to Allen's services, requiring the building of a much larger brick church in 1805. In 1817, Allen broke from the white-dominated Methodist Episcopal Church to found the black Christian denomination that would become the largest of its kind in the world: the African Methodist Episcopal Church (AME).

The present Mother Bethel AME Church, located in an area of the city revived from decay in recent decades by the restoration of many late eighteenth- and early nineteenth-century houses, is the fourth to be built on the original site purchased by Richard Allen. His tomb and a small museum with a bas relief by Henry Ossawa Tanner, one of the most accomplished black artists of the nineteenth century, are in the basement of the church.

FORT MOULTRIE NATIONAL MONUMENT

1214 Middle St. (Visitors Center)
Sullivan's Island
Charleston, SC 29428
843-883-3123
www.nps.gov/fomo
NPS

Enslaved Africans, hired from their masters in 1776, worked with white artisans to construct the squat, double-walled Fort Moultrie from thousands of palmetto trees and tons of shoveled sand on Sullivan's Island, which guarded the entrance into the harbor of Charleston. On June 28, 1776, just a week before the Declaration of Independence was signed, South Carolinians withstood the fierce bombardment of four attacking British ships and returned fire so effectively that the English withdrew with heavy casualties. The British were astounded at the ability of the fort to absorb the thousands of cannonballs fired during the ten-hour seige. When they returned in 1780 to overwhelm the fort at last, a British commander, Major Patrick Ferguson, described the slave-built fort as "the strongest Fort ever built by Hands."

Rented out by their masters to work on the fort, Charleston's slaves bolstered the feeling that the Americans could oppose the mighty British military machine. The battle at Sullivan's Island helped keep a key Southern port in patriot hands for almost four years. Yet enslaved Carolinians used every opportunity to secure their freedom by fleeing to the British. They did so by the thousands after the British seized the city in May 1780. Many of the slaves who had helped construct Fort Moultrie now fought on the other side of the war. When the British evacuated Charleston in December 1782, more than 5,200 former slaves went with them.

After the Revolution, Fort Moultrie became an important part of the new nation's coastal defense system, the sentinel guarding against British or French marauders. Black Carolinians provided labor and artisanal skills in rebuilding the fort again and again after ravaging hurricanes in 1783, 1804, 1809, 1813, and 1830. In 1860, Federal troops at Fort Moultrie moved to the protection of nearby Fort Sumter as the first bombardment of the Civil War began.

John and Abigail Adams House, Adams National Historic Park

Quincy, Mass.

Women and the American Revolution

This contemporary photograph shows a much larger house than Abigail Adams ever knew. Some of the furnishings were sent from London after she accompanied her husband there in 1784–85. Three generations of Adamses—John, John Quincy, and Charles Francis—served as diplomats abroad, and the furnishings of nearly every room of the Adams House bears testimony to this.

I long to hear that you have declared an independancy," Abigail Adams wrote from Braintree (now Quincy), Massachusetts, where she was managing the family farm and tending her young children, "and by the way in the code of laws which I suppose it will be necessary for you to make I desire you would remember the ladies, and be more generous and favorable to them than your ancestors." Abigail was addressing her husband, John, a Massachusetts lawyer and delegate to the Second Continental Congress meeting in Philadelphia. "Do not put such unlimited power into the hands of the husbands. Remember, all men would be tyrants if they could." Speaking the language of the decade-long argument between the colonies and England, Abigail punctuated her message: "If particular care and attention is not paid to the ladies, we are determined to foment a rebellion, and will not hold ourselves bound by any laws in which we have no voice, or representation." This was the clarion voice of one of the "founding mothers" who indelibly affected the course of the American Revolution.

John and Abigail Adams House, Adams National Historical Park

133 Franklin Street
Quincy, MA 02169
617-770-1175

www.nps.gov/adam
NRIS 66000051
NPS

DATE BUILT
1681

SIGNIFICANCE
This was Abigail Smith Adams's first home after she wed John Adams in 1764 and the home where she gave birth to five children. One of the most engaged women of the revolutionary era, Adams managed the house and farm for most of the years when her husband was in Philadelphia, New York, The Hague, London, and Paris.

After twenty-year-old Abigail Smith took the hand of John Adams in marriage in 1764, she moved into the house where her husband had been born and raised. This small frame and clapboard house looked much like thousands of other simple New England farmhouses. It had a central chimney with a ground-floor room on each side of it, two second-floor rooms, and an added, shed-like kitchen and back room. John Adams's father, Deacon John Adams, had purchased the house in 1720 from William Needham, when the building was already about forty years old, along with seven acres of land. When he died in 1761, Deacon Adams left it to his second son, Peter Boylston Adams, who sold it to John and Abigail in 1774. But for their first ten years together, Abigail and John rented the house and farmed the land while John pursued his career as a lawyer. Here Abigail delivered five children in the first seven years of her marriage; here she raised the family, managed the farm, and involved herself in the epochal events of the revolutionary era while her husband was away in Philadelphia as a member of the two Continental Congresses and as the new nation's emissary to the Netherlands, England, and France.

The Adamses' house, far smaller than today's much-rebuilt and extended version, bustled with activity. In autumn, she supervised hired hands haying, turning, and manuring the fields; coating the pastures with seaweed ox-carted from the shore; pressing apples into cider; mulching asparagus rows; stocking the cold house for the winter; mending the fences; and rebuilding walls. In spring, she saw that the crops were properly planted and weeded, the orchards stripped of caterpillars, the meadows ditched. "I shall be quite a Farmeriss [in] an other year," she told John proudly in 1776. And inside the house, she lived elbow to elbow with her four children, a domestic servant, and a farm worker. Together they occupied the sitting room, two upstairs chambers, and a small room in the lean-to.

During the British occupation of Boston in 1775, Abigail took in a family that fled the city, even after the farm worker whose tiny room they were to occupy refused to give it up and vowed that "cannon Ball shall not move him." At the same time, her house provided a welcome in July of that year to Generals George Washington and Charles Lee, along with their aides-de-camp, who came to pay their respects and sip the coffee Abigail provided.

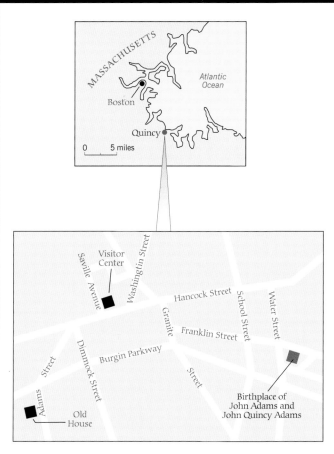

Through the war years, the house served as a spin-ning factory with Abigail providing homespun clothes for her children; a schoolhouse where she taught her children to read and write; and "an hospital in every part," as she wrote John, when a dysentery epidemic ravaged the town in August 1775, killing John's brother and Abigail's mother. And the house became a lying-in hospital when Abigail delivered their fifth child in July 1777—a "very fine Babe," she wrote her husband, but tragically, a still-born daughter who "never opened its Eyes in this world. . . . as tho they were only closed for sleep."

Even with the challenges of managing the house, farm, and family for most of the war without her hus-band, Abigail wrote scores of long letters to him and kept herself fully abreast of the war's progress. Extra-ordinarily capable, resourceful, and outspoken, she stood in the vanguard of those who believed with Thomas Paine that "the birthday of a new world was at hand." Many women were less ready than her to advance women's rights, including the right to vote, but she was by no means alone in pushing her well-placed

The Power of the Consumer: Women Shoppers Rebel

 Abigail Adams was a voracious reader, an astute commentator on public events, and an inexhaustible letter writer. In a letter to her husband, who was sitting with the Continental Congress in Philadelphia, she described a scene that put Boston's women at the center of the action on the homefront of the revolution. On a warm afternoon in July 1777, after the British army had moved south from Boston, a crowd of determined women gathered outside the warehouse of merchant Thomas Boylston. Many were shopkeepers who sold "necessaries" such as coffee, sugar, and flour to Boston's ordinary householders. A woman named Mrs. Colter was their spokesperson. She was firm that Boylston's control of the city's supply of coffee, which he was selling at a frightful price, was unacceptable—an act of great disservice to the community where the poor struggled to put a meal on the table. Abigail described the scene to her husband in vivid terms.

I have nothing new to entertain you with, unless it is an account of a new set of mobility [a mob] which have lately taken the lead in Boston. You must know that there is a great scarcity of sugar and coffee, articles which the female part of the state are very loth to give up, especially whilst they consider the scarcity occasioned by the merchants having secreted a large quantity. There has been much rout and noise in the town for several weeks. Some stores have been opened by a number of people and the coffee and sugar carried into the market and dealt out by pounds. It was rumoured that an eminent, wealthy, stingy merchant (who is a bachelor) had a hogshead of coffee in his store which he refused to sell to the committee under 6 shillings per pound. A number of females, some say a hundred, some say more, assembled with a cart and trucks, marched down to the warehouse, and demanded the keys, which he refused to deliver, upon which one of them seized him by his neck and tossed him into the cart. Upon his finding no quarter, he delivered the keys, when they topped up the cart and discharged him, then opened the warehouse, hoisted out the coffee themselves, put it into the trucks, and drove off. It was reported that he had a spanking among them, but this I believe was not true. A large concourse of men stood amazed silent spectators of the whole transaction.

With a powder horn in her right hand and rifle in her left, this "daughter of liberty" in Marblehead, Massachusetts, wears the male tricornered hat, ready to defend herself and her new nation. This woodcut by an anonymous artist was published in 1779.

husband toward new ways of thinking about how family relations as well as national affairs ought to be conducted. When John read her comments that women would not subscribe to laws in which they had no role in creating, he taunted her:

> As to your extraordinary code of laws, I cannot but laugh. We have been told that our struggle has loosened the bonds of government everywhere. That children and apprentices were disobedient—that schools and colleges were grown turbulent—that Indians slighted their guardians and Negroes grew insolent to their masters. But your letter was the first intimation that another tribe more numerous and powerful than all the rest were grown discontented. . . . Depend upon it, we know better than to repeal our masculine systems.

To that, Abigail promptly responded:

> Whilst you are proclaiming peace and good will to men, emancipating all nations, you insist upon retaining an absolute power over wives. But you must remember that arbitrary power is like most other things which are very hard, very liable to be broken. . . . We have it in our power not only to free ourselves but to subdue our masters, and without violence thrown both your natural and legal authority at our feet.

If not challenging "arbitrary power" so directly as Abigail, women in all parts of the rebellious colonies stepped into public spaces to play important roles in the Revolution that gave them greater legitimacy—as something more than the dependents of fathers, husbands, and brothers. In the years of protest against British revenue policies, women became essential in maintaining boycotts of imported British goods, in swearing off tea as a tainted imported commodity, and in spinning and weaving cloth to take the place of boycotted English cloth. Once the war was underway, women provided indispensable services. Some women became spies—on both sides of the Revolution. By night, Lydia Darragh, a middle-aged Quaker teacher's wife, served evening meals to British officers occupying Philadelphia in 1777–78; by day, she smuggled messages sewed into the linings of her pockets. What she overheard as the British discussed

their spring campaign plans over dinner reached George Washington at Valley Forge.

Many more women—as many as 20,000 according to one careful estimate—traveled with the armies, cooking, cleaning, nursing, and comforting the men. Some even accompanied their husbands into battle, loading guns and attending the wounded. Sometimes acting as informal commissaries, they scoured the countryside for food, forage, and clothes. In the winter of 1777–78, farmer's wife Mary Frazier, as her granddaughter later recounted,

> day after day collected from neighbors and friends far and near, whatever they could spare for the comfort of the destitute soldiers, the blankets, and yarn and half worn clothing thus obtained she brought to her own house, where they would be patched and darned and made wearable and comfortable. . . . She often sat up half the night, sometimes all, to get clothing ready. Then with it, and whatever could be obtained for food, she would have packed on her horse and set out on her cold lonely journey to the camp—which she went to repeatedly during the winter.

Mercy Otis Warren, Penwoman of the Revolution

Mercy Otis Warren, like her close friend Abigail Adams, was drawn to politics. She wielded a potent pen and carved new spaces in the public arena for women. Mercy had access to the deliberations of Massachusetts revolutionary politics because her brother, James Otis, and her husband, James Warren, were closely tied to Boston inner circles where John and Samuel Adams figured importantly.

Boston's premier portraitist, John Singleton Copley, captured Mercy Otis Warren, mother of three sons, at age thirty-five. Close to John and Abigail Adams, she often argued with them and even offended John with critical comments about him in her history of the American Revolution.

In the years leading up to the war, when many radical strategy sessions were held in her home, she emerged as one of the patriots' most effective propagandists. In the early 1770s, she stepped into a male realm, filling the Massachusetts newspapers with satiric poems and plays. Satirizing Lieutenant Governor Thomas Hutchinson, upholder of British policies, as "Rapatio, Bashaw of Servia," who aimed to crush "the ardent love of liberty in Servia's free-born sons" and lampooning other Crown defenders as "Beau Trumps," "Hum Humbug," "Brigadier Hateall," and "Sir Spendall," Warren fueled the opposition to English policies.

After the war, Mercy Warren remained a force in politics through her writings. In 1788, she published spirited attacks on the Constitution as its ratification was being debated in Massachusetts. Warren argued that the Constitution betrayed revolutionary principles by vesting too much power in the executive branch and unduly limiting rights that belonged to the states. In 1791, she wrote warmly in defense of the American Revolution and in 1805 published a three-volume history of the American Revolution. This book strained her friendship with Abigail Adams because she portrayed John Adams unfavorably for his aristocratic and excessively pro-British leanings and as having "forgotten the principles of the American Revolution" during his tenure as the new nation's second President.

At the climactic battle at Yorktown, Virginia, in 1781, Sarah Osborn, wife of a New York blacksmith cooked and washed for the American troops and brought them food under fire because, as she remarked to Washington, "it would not do for the men to fight and starve too." She was there to witness the British lay down their arms and strike their colors.

Off the battlefield, women like Abigail Adams were central to the effort to redesign the political culture of a democratizing society. Most reformers who argued the necessity of public education for a self-governing republic considered women as vital in shaping a republic of educated, thoughtful, involved citizens. Women drawn into a central role as consumers with the power of the boycott played an early part in this process of drawing apolitical people into a public dialogue. Another part of the process was women's participation in street demonstrations to heckle and shame violators of community-sworn compacts to end importation of British goods. Women also became a special part of the society's moral force by encouraging men to go into battle, often shaming men to fight in the interest of the state. Writing plays to whip up patriotism, as did Abigail Adams's friend Mercy Otis Warren, put women in the public eye in yet another way. Although not openly empowered, women found their own particular ways to contribute to the war effort, give aid to their fellow rebels, and bring down the British.

THE OLD HOUSE

Adams National Historic Park
135 Adams Street
Quincy, MA 02169
617-770-1175
www.nps.gov/adam
NPS

Abigail and John Adams purchased the Quincy, Massachusetts, house on what is now Adams Street in 1787, when Adams was the U.S. envoy to England and Abigail traveled to England to be with him. It would remain the homestead for four generations of one of the most famous American families. Built in 1731, only a short distance from the Adamses' former home, the house now stands in a densely residential area. Originally constructed as a two-story clapboard frame house with an attic, it was not large enough for Abigail's liking. "In height and breadth," she wrote her daughter Nabby, "it feels like a wren's house." Nabby should come to the house with no feathers on her hat, and her husband no heels on his shoes, for the low ceilings would not permit it, she joked. But after their return from England, Abigail and John began extensive renovations. In 1797, when Adams returned to Philadelphia to serve as the second President of the United States, Abigail oversaw the addition of a large L-shaped wing that nearly doubled the house size and provided a large library for the Adamses' extensive collection of books. As during the Revolution, Abigail managed the family farm.

Four generations of the Adams family lived in the "Old House." Abigail Adams found the house to be too small for her liking and had it enlarged many times.

Abigail Adams's first son, John Quincy Adams, became Secretary of State under President James Monroe and later was elected the nation's sixth President. He renovated the house extensively in 1829 and 1836 to use as his summer home. After the Civil War, Abigail's grandson, Charles Francis Adams made further renovations and additions, including a new three-story addition as servants' quarters. The large house with seven bays across the front facade is the result of this further upgrading—a far cry from the "wren's house" that Abigail first saw in 1787. Charles Francis Adams also built a separate library of stone and brick and a carriage house while converting a working farm into a Victorian country gentleman's seat. The Adams home became a National Historic Site in 1972.

BENJAMIN FRANKLIN HOUSE

Franklin Court
Philadelphia, PA 19106
NHL

Sarah Franklin Bache, the daughter of Benjamin and Deborah Franklin, was one year older than Abigail Adams and was part of the cohort of revolutionary-era women who assumed active roles in public affairs. She, her husband, and their growing brood of children lived in her parents' Philadelphia house during the Revolution. The house was sited in the middle of a courtyard on Market Street, only a few blocks from the Delaware River. The capacious, three-story brick house was open to the light on all four sides. An arched carriageway brought Franklin, his family, and a constant stream of visitors into the spacious court. Here, Sarah Franklin Bache developed a keen political consciousness that turned her into one of the Revolution's most active women.

Sarah fled from her father's house in the face of the British occupation of Philadelphia in September 1777. Four years into the war, she stepped forward to organize Philadelphia women in a house-to-house campaign to raise money for General George Washington's revenue-starved army. Obtaining $300,000 in pledges, Sarah Bache, at Washington's suggestion, bought linen for shirts, which scores of women cut and sewed into 2,000 shirts.

Shortly, an essayist in the *Pennsyvania Packet,* calling herself only "Debora," wrote that "it must strike the enemy as with an apoplexy, to be informed, that the women of America are attentive to the wants of the Soldiery." If women in other cities would follow the example of Sarah Bache and her compatriots, wrote Debora, "the women will reinspire the war; and ensure, finally, victory and peace." Sarah presided over the tea table as her father's hostess for the last five years of his life. When the Constitutional Convention met in the summer of 1787, she was a busy manager of Franklin's house as Washington and other leaders came to pay respects and discuss the proceedings of the momentous convention.

Franklin's home and its contents received little respect from his heirs. After he died in 1790, Sarah Bache's family moved to the "suburbs" and rented the house out; later it was a boardinghouse. They auctioned off valuable furniture, silverware, Franklin's harpsichord, copying press, the "Franklin stoves" he had invented, and the sedan chair he used during his failing years. After Sarah's death her children tore down the house and sold the property to developers. A century and a half later, when Franklin Court became part of the Independence National Historical Park, Philadelphia architect Robert Venturi created steel tubular frames giving a hypothetical, three-dimensional outline to the house where Sarah Bache Franklin had spent the last years of her life.

WEST POINT MILITARY RESERVATION

U.S. Military Academy
West Point, NY 10996
www.usma.edu
NHL

The Revolutionary War fortifications first constructed between 1775 and 1778 off Constitution Island to control the lower Hudson River became part of the site of the U.S. Military Academy established by Congress in 1802. (The academy's more familiar name, "West Point," derives from its position on the western shore of the island.) Some of the redoubts and stone ramparts constructed in the rocky hills above

the river have survived and have been stabilized. As the main source of its army leadership, West Point has been associated with American military strength for two centuries.

Two women famous for their revolutionary military exploits knew West Point well. Accompanying her husband, a private in the Pennsylvania Regiment of Artillery, Margaret Corbin stood under fire and helped her husband swab a cannon bore, rammed the gun with shot, and took over the gun when enemy fire killed him. She survived grapeshot wounds that maimed her arm. Assigned to the Invalid Regiment at West Point, she remained in the area after the war, living on one of the first pensions given an American war widow. For years, known as "Captain Molly," she roamed the Hudson River waterfront dressed in an old artillery coat and vest. In 1926, Corbin was reinterred with military honors in the cemetery at West Point, near the Old Cadet Chapel.

Even more spectacular was Deborah Sampson's career. Descended from Pilgrim colony leaders William Bradford, John Alden, and Miles Standish, Sampson grew up on a Massachusetts farm where she developed stature, strength, and stamina unusual for women in this era. At age twenty, she enlisted as a man but was discharged when her true identity was discovered. Trekking to Boston, she enlisted again in 1782 in the Continental Army. After marching ten days to West Point, her regiment saw action against the British near White Plains and then in Tarrytown, New York, where she was wounded in battle. A year later, hospitalized with a raging fever in Philadelphia, her gender was discovered and she was discharged just after the articles of peace were signed.

Sampson obtained a war pension in 1792, and her exploits led to a lecture tour where she entertained audiences with her wartime heroics. Taking the stage in her blue and white uniform, she shouldered her musket, ran through twenty-seven maneuvers of the Manual of Arms Exercise, and then gave a rousing speech. Reverting to a feminine demeanor, she admitted her rashness as "a foible, an error and presumption." But she still stood proudly behind her decision to fight alongside the American "avengers of the wrong" against the English who had tried "to enforce on us plans of subjugation." Until her death in 1827, she spoke knowledgeably on military tactics, politics, and religion.

MONMOUTH BATTLEFIELD STATE PARK

347 Freehold-Englishtown Road
Manalapan, NJ 07726
732-462-9616
www.state.nj.us/dep/forestry/parks/monbat.htm
NHL

Monmouth Battlefield State Park, comprising about 1,200 acres, preserves a Revolutionary War landscape of woods, hedgerows, wetlands, fields, and orchards. Here an important battle occurred on June 28, 1778, the last big military engagement in the north, when the Americans attacked the British army, which had evacuated Philadelphia and was retreating across New Jersey to British-occupied New York City. Today, the New Jersey Historic Trust is using contemporary maps, physical evidence, and battle accounts to return the battlefield to the way it appeared in 1778. Over time, swampy creek beds have been drained, rough ravines graded, and a railroad and highway constructed across the battlefield. Only on a scorching summer day can the visitor conceive of the battle that occurred on a day so oppressively hot that as many (including George Washington's horse) died of heat exhaustion as of battle wounds.

More vivid in the American consciousness than the battle itself was the heroism under fire of Mary Ludwig Hays. Married to a gunner in a Pennsylvania artillery regiment, Sergeant John Caspar Hays, Mary accompanied her husband through seven years of war. Joseph Martin, a soldier at Monmouth, described her in his diary as a formidable woman "who smoked, chewed tobacco and swore like a trooper." She was hauling buckets of water to the artillery soldiers on June 28 when she found her husband lying wounded by his cannon. Taking his place, she loaded and fired the cannon. Many other women, who became known as "Molly Pitchers" in Mary's honor (as Molly is a nickname for Mary), carried water to quench their husbands' thirst and cool the cannons.

When a battle ended, they remained in camp, cooking meals, tending fires, binding wounds, washing and mending shirts, and lifting morale. These were the "camp followers" of the Revolution—who were mostly with the army not to do battle but to do service. Many years later, remarried after her husband's death, Mary Hays McCauley received a federal pension for her wartime service.

A Connecticut private present at the Battle of Monmouth recorded that he had seen a British cannonball fly directly between Mary Hays's legs when she was reaching for a cartridge, "without doing any other damage than carrying away all the lower part of her petticoat." Unflustered, he noted, she continued firing with the comment "that it was lucky [the shell] did not pass a little higher, for in that case it might have carried away something else."

Johnson Hall

Johnstown, N.Y.

The Native American Revolution

Sir William Johnson presents medals to Iroquois chiefs in 1772 in this painting by Edward Lamson Henry. The artist's attention to historical details makes this representation of the house and flanking buildings realistic, although the orderliness of the meeting is probably exaggerated.

Johnson Hall, the largest structure on New York's eighteenth-century frontier, was a nerve center for conducting Native American affairs in eastern North America during the late colonial period. It became a strategic site for decision making among Native Americans regarding their involvement in the Revolution. At the center of these diplomatic relations was the Johnson family, father and son, who played critical roles in Iroquois political and military affairs. Sir William Johnson, the father, was the most important figure in American Indian–white relations in eastern North America for many years. Born in Ireland, he emigrated in 1738 to New York, where he settled in the Mohawk River Valley. Here he hunted, traded, and lived with the Mohawk for many years, dressing like them, participating in their war dances, smoking pipes at their councils, and taking the Mohawk name of Warraghiyagey (meaning "man who does much business"). "Something in his natural temper," observed Cadwallader Colden, a physician and writer on Indian affairs "responds to Indian ways."

For some 200,000 Native Americans living east of the Mississippi River, the American Revolution was as much a time to "try men's souls" as it was for the colonists. With the war approaching, Native Americans found themselves wooed by both revolutionaries and British, for both sides knew that Indian military prowess could be a deciding factor. How would the dozens of Indian nations decide? Around campfires and village clearings, every tribe had to search the past, evaluate the present, and plot a course for the future.

At the heart of the Native American strategy during the Revolution were the twin goals of political independence and territorial defense. Ironically, most native groups concluded that *their* revolutionary goals could best be achieved by fighting *against* the side that proclaimed the equality of all men, the colonial rebels. That would ally the natives with the British, the side that the colonists accused of trampling their natural irreducible rights. The logic of nearly 200 years of abrasive contact with colonizing Europeans compelled the choice, for the settler-subjects of the English king most threatened Native American autonomy, while royal power, before the Revolution, had attempted to protect Indian lands from white encroachment.

Johnson Hall, one mile northwest of present-day Johnstown, New York, in the Mohawk River Valley, was the center of William Johnson's Native American empire. The scene at the site was buzzing with activity in 1763 after Johnson hired Samuel Fuller, a local contractor, to build his house. Fuller assembled several dozen woodcutters, carpenters, and stone masons to fell trees, fashion them into beams and planking, frame the house, and finish its interior and exterior at breakneck speed in the spring and summer of 1763.

The carpenters grooved wooden blocks to look like stone for the exterior siding and added handsome architectural touches in the rooflines as well as carved detailing on the entrance porch. Following the tradition of baronial houses in England, Johnson designed a central hall on each of its two floors, large enough to drive a horse and sleigh through. On both floors, two large, eighteen-by-eighteen-foot rooms flank the central hall, with smaller rooms behind each of them. Impressive chimneys serve all the rooms, while a broad staircase with carved mahogany rails and balusters added to the

Johnson Hall

Hall Avenue
Johnstown, NY 12095
518-762-8712

NRIS 66000520
NHL

DATE BUILT
1763

ORIGINAL OWNER
William Johnson

SIGNIFICANCE
Johnson Hall, built in 1763, was the baronial mansion of Sir William Johnson, British Northern Superintendent of Indian Affairs from 1754 to 1774. Johnson Hall became a vital location for American Indian leaders to meet and therefore to decide the stance that Indian nations would take in relation to the American Revolution.

grandeur of Johnson Hall. In the blue parlor on the first floor, seven large paintings in gilt frames portrayed England's King George III and the rest of the royal family.

Appointed royal Superintendent of Indian Affairs in the Northern Colonies, Johnson meant the hall to symbolize the hospitality he wished to extend to visiting Indian leaders on the New York frontier. At the same time, it indicated the power of the region's largest landowner and Indian trader, as well as the man in whom the king's authority was invested. The large house was built of wood but made to look like stone, making it all the more impressive. Measuring fifty-five feet in length, it was flanked by two stone buildings that served various purposes—all situated on eighteen acres.

The furnishings of Johnson Hall reflected the rich hospitality that Johnson extended to visitors who came to his wilderness capital, "from all parts of America, from Europe, and from the West Indies," as one visitor described it, where "all were equally and hospitably entertained." A 100-pound dinner bell called guests to a long walnut table and leather-bottomed walnut chairs, silver dinner service, and drinking glasses and decanters. After bountiful meals, guests could enjoy the backgammon and card tables, billiards, and ninepins. Johnson also furnished his mansion so he could offer sleeping accommodations to overnight guests. The bedrooms had four-poster beds with feather mattresses and buffalo-skin blankets. Even the parlors had cots in them.

William Johnson's house may not have looked so neat and clean in the years before the American Revolution, certainly not when it teemed with farmers, traders, tradesmen, visiting Indian chiefs, and a brood of children.

Samson Occum, Indian Town Founder and Revolutionary War Neutral

Born in 1723, Samson Occum became a Christianized Mohegan after his mother converted to Christianity when the boy was thirteen years old. He studied at Reverend Eleazar Wheelock's famous Christian school—later to become Dartmouth College—where he learned Greek, Latin, Hebrew, and English. In 1747, he received a Presbyterian license to preach, becoming one of 133 Indian preachers in New England. Two years later, at age twenty-six, Occum became minister and teacher at Montauk, an Indian village on the eastern end of Long Island, New York. He married a Montauk woman and had ten children with her. For two years in the 1770s, Occum traveled through England preaching hundreds of sermons to raise money for the new Native American school that Wheelock intended to build. Returning to New England as the American Revolution broke out, Occum decided to establish a self-governing Christian community for Indians far from corrupting white influence. Obtaining a tract of land from the Oneida in central New York, he called the community Eeayam Quittoowauconnuck (which means "Brothertown" in English).

Brothertown lay in one of the fiercest war zones of the American Revolution, and this forced Occum to seek refuge in Stockbridge, Massachusetts. With his Christian converts, he joined many of the people from his tribe. For a time, he returned to his Connecticut

In this portrait Samson Occom is wearing the typical clerical garb of black cloth and white bib. He became disillusioned in his last years after Dartmouth College cut back its admission of native students. Rather than alma mater, he said, it had become alba mater (White Mother).

home, where he urged Indians to remain neutral in the "white man's war." Occum returned to Brothertown after the war and became the spiritual leader of this growing community of Indians seeking some way of maintaining themselves independently among the victorious white Americans. He remained the leader of Brothertown until his death in 1792.

If Johnson Hall was designed with hospitality in mind, its layout also reflected the social hierarchy of one of eighteenth-century New York's most extensive families. One of the two stone blockhouses built in 1764, connected by a tunnel to the basement of the mansion, provided quarters for Johnson's numerous indentured servants and slaves, the latter numbering as many as twenty at one time. His indentured servants included a blind Irish harpist, a German butler, and an Indian boy dressed in livery. The overseer of his plantation had a one-room stone house of his own, while stables for horses, coops for hens and peacocks, cages for monkeys, and kennels for dogs accommodated the animal residents of Johnson Hall. Crude wooden buildings served to accommodate visiting Native Americans. And a large Council House, 30 feet by 100 feet was erected about 300 yards from the mansion.

Johnson Hall was the site of repeated councils with Iroquois chiefs from its completion in 1763 until Johnson's death in 1774. On the spacious lawn in front of the house, Sir William dispensed gifts from the British government. On treaty days and gift-giving days, he staged elaborate fairs with Indian dancing, greased pig contests, and sack races. "All the Nations present [were] assembled in my new House," he wrote in 1763.

Today, visitors stroll on well-tended grass, view the house in orderly condition, and hear nothing but English spoken. But 250 years ago it was not like this at all. Johnson described one group of Mohawks "being ready to depart assembled in the Summer house in the Garden, and ten of their Warriors being naked, painted and feather'd . . . marched in Slow order in two Ranks, singing their Song according to the Ottawa Custom." At Johnson Hall a babel of languages, dialects, and accents mingled as Scots-Irish, Dutch, Germans, African Americans, English, French, Welsh, and Swiss participated in parleying, trading, and socializing. Some were Catholic, others were Anglican or Presbyterian, still others were Moravian, Lutheran, or German Reformed. Indian visitors were Iroquoian-speaking Mohawk, Seneca, and Oneida; Algonquian-speaking Delaware and Shawnee; and many others who often spoke languages that may have been from the same linguistic roots, but were not mutually understandable. People's dress varied almost as much as their tongues.

Social arrangements at Johnson Hall were dictated by Johnson's two common-law marriages (which were not unusual on the New York frontier). In several bedrooms slept the three children of Catherine (Catty) Weisenberg, a slender, dark-eyed runaway indentured servant from Germany whom Johnson had taken as a housekeeper and consort in 1739. Weisenberg had died four years before Johnson Hall was built, but her first child, Nancy, replaced her as Johnson Hall's housekeeper.

In the same year that Weisenberg died, the forty-four-year-old Johnson took a second common-law wife—twenty-three-year-old Degonwadonti, or Molly Brant as she would come to be known. Midway through the Seven Years War of 1756–63, in which the British and their American colonists fought the French and their Indian allies, Johnson met Molly. According to some accounts, she was the daughter of an important Mohawk chief and granddaughter of one of the famous "Four Indian Kings" who traveled to London in 1710 to negotiate with Queen Anne about an Iroquois alliance with the English against French Canada. Johnson's relationship with Molly Brant lasted until his death, just before the American Revolution. Sometimes called "the brown Lady Johnson," she and her common-law husband raised three of their mixed-race children at

William Johnson signed this treaty with Delaware, Shawnee, and Mingo chiefs on July 13, 1765. Indian chiefs used pictographs (small drawings) to sign the treaty. At the top left is the pictograph signature of Delaware chief Turtle Heart.

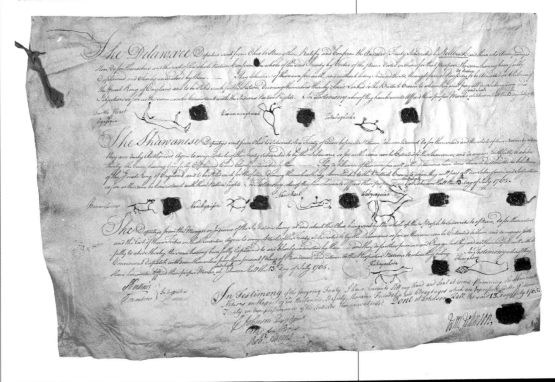

Johnson Hall, as well as two other children Johnson fathered with other Mohawk women who have never been identified.

Molly Brant's brother, Joseph Brant—known to Indians as Thayendanegea—was a frequent visitor to Johnson Hall and became a key figure in the natives' American Revolution. Bilingual and bicultural, Brant had fought with the Americans against the French in the Seven Years War. He aided the colonists again by battling the Ottawa leader Pontiac's insurgents who tried to expel the British soldiers and their encroaching American cousins from the Ohio country in 1763, after the Indians had lost their French allies in the Seven Years' War (1756-1763). But with the storm clouds gathering between England and the American colonies, Brant realized that the Iroquois would be greatly threatened by an American victory. Therefore, he sailed to London in 1775 to see what the king would offer the Iroquois for their support.

Brant returned to New York a few weeks after the Declaration of Independence was signed in Philadelphia and immediately served with British General George Howe at Long Island in the first major defeat of George

Washington's army. Then, in November 1776, he traveled by foot and canoe through the lands of the Iroquois and their Indian allies in the Ohio country to spread the message that "their own country and liberty were in danger from the rebels." Brant's diplomatic mission was crucial in bringing most of the Iroquois into the war on the British side in the summer of 1777.

Sir William Johnson died in 1774, shortly before Brant went to London, but his son, later knighted as Sir John Johnson, took over his father's role and became the lord of Johnson Hall. Brant worked with John Johnson, who fled to Canada in May 1776, throughout the war.

In the interior of eastern North America, most Native American nations followed the Iroquois' lead in siding with the British. The Shawnee in the Ohio country and the Cherokee of the upper South allied to attack the encroaching Virginians even before the Continental Congress declared independence. "From being a great nation," the Shawnee sorrowfully told the Cherokee in May 1776, "[we are now] reduced to a handful." Knowing that the white settlers intended to destroy them, the Shawnee argued that it was "better to die like men than to dwindle away by inches." Two months later, the Cherokee, led by Dragging Canoe, a young militant Cherokee chief, attacked white settlements on the Virginia, Carolina, and Georgia frontiers. They were trying to drive out encroaching settlers who had ignored the English Proclamation Line of 1763 that forbade white settlement west of the Appalachian Mountain crest line.

For five years, the kind of frontier warfare that devastated both white and Iroquois settlements in central New York was repeated on the southern frontier. Although never militarily defeated during the war, the Iroquois lost about one-third of their people and were abandoned by their British allies at the peace talks in Paris. When the British finally recognized American independence and conceded defeat in 1783, they acknowledged American sovereignty over the vast part of the continent east of the Mississippi River from the Great Lakes to Florida. Much of this territory was still occupied by the Native American allies of the British.

The Indians were left to cope with aggressive, combat-experienced, and land-hungry Americans. Regarding the Indians as defeated enemies, the Americans showed little mercy. From their point of view, the Indians had forfeited

A Johnson Hall Intimate Raises the Indian Standard of War

 At the principal Cherokee town of Chota (located in what is today eastern Tennessee) in May 1776, American Indian leaders from a dozen nations met to discuss strategy in the war already underway between England and its colonists. Henry Stuart, a British agent to the Cherokee, was present and reported in a letter to his brother, the British government's Superintendent of Indian Affairs on the decision to pass the war belt from nation to nation.

The standard of war was erected, the flag staff and posts of the town house were painted black and red . . . The principal deputy for the Mohawks and Six Nations began. He produced a belt of white and purple wampum [and] said he supposed there was not a man present that could not read his talk; the back settlers of the northern provinces whom he termed the Long Knife had without any provocation come into one of their towns and murdered their people and the son of their Great Beloved Man; [This rumor that William Johnson's son had been murdered was false]. that what was their case one day might be the case of another nation another day; that his nation was fighting at this time and that he was sent by them to secure the friendship of all nations for he considered their interests as one, and that at this time they should forget all their quarrels among themselves and turn their eyes and their thoughts one way. . . . The principal deputy of the Ottawas produced a white belt with some purple figures; they expressed their desire of confirming a lasting bond of true friendship with all their red brethren; that they were almost constantly at war one nation against another and reduced by degrees, while their common enemies were taking the advantage of their situation . . . The [war] belt was received by Chincanacina. It was some minutes before anyone got up to give his assent which was to be done by laying hold of the belt. At last a head man . . . who had lived long in the Mohawk Nation and whose wife had constantly lived in Sir William Johnson's house was the first who rose up to take the belt. . . . He sung the war song and all the Northern Indians joined in the chorus. Almost all the young warriors from the different parts of the Nation followed his example, though many of them expressed their uneasiness at being concerned in a war against the white people.

their land and their political autonomy. Confronting insurmountable odds and thunderstruck that the British sold them out to their American enemies, tribal leaders were forced to relinquish enormous tracts of land to the victorious Americans and to agree to treaties that confined them to specified reservation areas— islands within their former empires. Joseph Brant, like many other native leaders who fought on the British side, was enraged to be betrayed by "our allies for whom we have so often freely bled." He spent the last twenty years of his life trying to help the Iroquois adjust to the harsh new realities that came with the American victory.

Mohawk chief Joseph Brant was a powerful Indian leader and respected on both sides of the Atlantic. Also known as Thayendanegea, Brant was the subject of more portraits than all but a few white revolutionary leaders.

The restoration of Johnson Hall began more than 100 years later, in 1906, when the State of New York acquired it from its private owners. Later work, beginning in the late 1950s after extensive archaeological research, has returned the house and its outbuildings to their eighteenth-century form by removing most of the Victorian details added in the nineteenth century and by reconstructing the outbuildings. Each room of the house is furnished with eighteenth-century furniture, native artifacts, paintings, and military weapons. A statue of Sir William Johnson, created in the early twentieth century, greets visitors approaching the house. A wooded park of 18 acres surrounds the mansion. "Molly Brant's Room" is on the second floor, and in the basement museum, visitors can watch "a musical evening at Johnson Hall in 1772." Sir William and his guests play assorted instruments while his faithful housekeeper, Molly Brant, sits with young children, who are alluded to as being Johnson's own.

ORISKANY BATTLEFIELD

7801 State Route 69
Oriskany, NY, 13424
315-768-7224
NHL

Just west of the town of Oriskany along the Mohawk River stands the Oriskany Battlefield. Today this is an eighty-seven-acre grassy, well-tended park, but at the time it was a thickly forested area. It was designated a New York State historic site in 1927 and a National Historic Landmark in 1963. Here on August 6, 1777, American militiamen fought against Iroquois warriors and their American Loyalist allies in an attempt to relieve the besieged Fort Stanwix (located in present-day Rome, New York), which controlled access to the western Mohawk Valley and the Great Lakes. The siege was conducted by Sir John Johnson and his uncle Joseph Brant with his Mohawk warriors.

Attempting to break this siege, 800 American militiamen recruited about sixty Oneida scouts from one of the two Iroquois nations that allied with the Americans. With some 900 Mohawk under his command, Joseph Brant ambushed the advancing American-Oneida relief column six miles from the fort, where the road passed through a ravine. In one of the fiercest battles of the war, both sides suffered heavy casualties. The Americans withdrew and the siege of Fort Stanwix continued until the end of August, when another relief column headed by Benedict Arnold succeeded in driving off the Mohawk-Loyalist besiegers.

MISSION HOUSE

Main Street
Stockbridge, MA 01262
413-298-3239
NHL

The Mission House built by Congregational minister John Sergeant in 1739 is typical of the colonial Massachusetts homestead—a sturdy two-story, rectangular frame-and-clapboard house with few frills but pleasing simplicity and symmetry. Before the American Revolution, Sergeant lived among and taught the Mahican people here in the western Massachusetts town of Stockbridge for fifteen years. Mastering their language, Sergeant preached every Sunday in their tongue as well as in English. He also translated English prayers and portions of the Bible into their language. When the American Revolution erupted, the Stockbridge Indians, as they came to be called, remained loyal to the Americans. Some fought with George Washington's troops at Boston in 1775 and later in New York, New Jersey, and Canada. But they returned from the battlefields to find that their American neighbors had taken over much of their land.

The Mission House has two interior chimneys, a center hall, and flanking kitchen and parlor on the first floor. Three bedrooms and a study occupy the second floor. A striking exterior feature is the double "Christian" doors with vertical panels carved with biblical themes and bracing in the shape of crosses. The house served as Reverend Sergeant's home and as a place to meet with the Mahicans, whose village lay below the hill on which the house was constructed. Sergeant family descendants lived in the house until 1879. In 1928, in a state of great decay, the mission house was purchased by Mabel Choate, a noted American lawyer, and was then dismantled and meticulously reconstructed nearly to its original state. The house is furnished with seventeenth- and eighteenth-century furniture and other household articles.

The Mahicans who frequently visited the Mission House benefited little from their allegiance to the Americans. After the war, their land threatened, the Mahicans moved west to live among the Oneida and later, in the early nineteenth century, were forced to move farther west to Indiana and later to Wisconsin.

NEWTOWN BATTLEFIELD

455 Oneida Road
Elmira, NY 14901
607-732-6067
NHL

The Iroquois forces led by Joseph Brant and Sir John Johnson had driven thousands of patriot farmers from the wheat and cattle belt in southern New York and northern Pennsylvania in the summer of 1778, depriving George Washington's army of much-needed provisions. To counter this, Washington launched a two-pronged invasion of Iroquois country to vanquish some 2,000 Iroquois warriors and protect the settlers' frontier from further Indian attacks. Led by Major General John Sullivan, one column of 2,400 men marched northward from Easton, Pennsylvania, while a second column of 1,400 men, led by Brigadier General James Clinton, moved west along the Mohawk River, then south down the Susquehanna River to meet up with Sullivan at Tioga. Pursuing a "scorched earth" policy of burning all Iroquois towns, orchards, fields, and stored food, Sullivan's men marched to the motto "Civilization or death to all American savages."

Newtown Battlefield was the site of one of the many skirmishes in the summer of 1779 between the Iroquois-British forces and the Americans. It is the one place during this long and costly campaign that all the contending leaders were present: Sullivan, Clinton, Brant, Johnson, and lesser officers. On August 29, 1779, near present-day Elmira, New York, and only one mile from the Indian village of Newtown, the Iroquois took a stand after retreating from their villages that the Americans had torched. In a three-hour battle, Brant led an attack on the New Hampshire brigade and coordinated a retreat of his forces after they failed to ambush the advancing Americans. Sullivan's army proceeded west two days later and reached the major Seneca town of Genesee, where the Iroquois had 128 log houses. Sullivan's uncontested army burned them all to the ground. By summer's end, Sullivan's march had scorched 41 Iroquois villages with some 650 log houses and 160,000 bushels of corn. A bitter winter followed. "We found that there was not a mouthful of any kind of sustenance left," wrote Mary Jemison, a white woman who lived with the Indians, "not even enough to keep a child one day from perishing with hunger."

FORT KLOCK

Route 5; 2 Miles East of St. Johnsville
St. Johnsville, NY 13452
518-568-7779
www.fortklock.com
NHL

Sir John Johnson and Joseph Brant, remaining uncowed by John Sullivan's "scorched earth" 1779 expedition, launched devastating attacks against the frontier towns of New York. In August and October 1780, two attacks targeted Fort Klock on the Mohawk River. Built in 1750 by Dutch settler, Johannes Klock, the fort was a typical Mohawk Valley outpost—a fortified house and fur-trading post, with massive stone walls nearly two feet thick and later surrounded by a log stockade. During the American Revolution it provided refuge for settlers who, facing raiding Iroquois and Tories, could fire muskets through loopholes on every side of the house.

In 1780, with a combined force of British regulars, colonial Loyalist "Greens," and a company of Hessians (German mercenary soldiers hired by the English), Sir John Johnson rendezvoused with several hundred Iroquois warriors led by Joseph Brant, the much-feared Mohawk leader, and Seneca chief Cornplanter. Burning houses, barns, and crops along their line of march in the Schoharie Valley, the British forces reached Fort Klock on October 19, 1780. After a spirited, indecisive fight, the Indians and British retreated. But before they left, they destroyed the houses of about 700 farmers and devastated their fields. By the end of 1781 the American population of the Mohawk Valley, a major breadbasket for the American cause, had been reduced from about 15,000 to 5,000.

The Fort Klock Restoration Committee rebuilt the badly decayed fort in the 1960s. Acquiring ten acres of land surrounding the fort, later expanded to thirty acres, the committee also reconstructed a schoolhouse and an adjacent blacksmith's shop. The fort has been restored to its original condition.

Old Saint Mary's Episcopal Church

Burlington, N.J.

Loyalists: The King's Friends

The interior of Old St. Mary's is a good example of the simplicity of eighteenth-century churches. The plain but sturdy pews were uncushioned, and undecorated interior beams added to the modesty of the sanctuary.

N early every Sunday, William Franklin, the royal governor of New Jersey, and his wife, Elizabeth, walked ceremoniously down the brick-paved Wood Street, passed through the tall, double doors of St. Mary's Episcopal Church in Burlington, New Jersey, and sat in the specially designated governor's pew. Founded in 1702 as the first mission church of the Society for the Propagation of the Gospel in Foreign Parts—the society devoted to spreading the Anglican faith in England's colonies—the church became the mother parish of the Anglican (later

Episcopal) Diocese of New Jersey. St. Mary's members revered the silver articles used for communion sent across the Atlantic Ocean by England's Queen Anne shortly after the church opened its doors, and they proudly worshiped in New Jersey's provincial capital. In the turbulent days leading toward the Declaration of Independence, this church was the gathering place of both the supporters and enemies of Franklin, a key figure among American loyalists. Loyalists were colonists who refused to join the independence movement and remained true to their king when the shooting began.

The congregants of St. Mary's Church found themselves deeply divided between patriots and loyalists during the American Revolution, as did the members of many other colonial churches. Governor William Franklin had inducted Jonathan Odell as the church's new minister in 1767, and Odell fully supported Franklin's loyalist philosophy. Standing under the British coat of arms in his powdered wig and scarlet robes of office, New Jersey's governor addressed the colony's council and assembly in the stone Burlington County courthouse, a short distance from St. Mary's, in January 1776. Reading private instructions from London, the governor firmly conveyed King George III's warning:

> His Majesty laments to find his subjects in America so lost to their true interests as neither to accept the resolution of the House of Commons . . . nor make it the basis of negotiation. As they have preferred engaging in a rebellion which menaces to overthrow the Constitution, it becomes his Majesty's duty . . . to reduce his rebellious subjects to obedience. . . . The commanders of His Majesty's squadrons in America have orders to proceed, as in the case of a town in actual rebellion.

The time was at hand, argued the governor, for New Jersey's assembly to ignore the rash, treasonous behavior of the Continental Congress in raising an army. Instead, the assembly should address the king directly, asking for a further attempt to reconcile the long-smoldering arguments between the Crown and the colonies. But how would the parishioners of St. Mary's Church respond? They knew that Burlington's mayor, John Lawrence, as well as their minister, Jonathan Odell, agreed with Franklin. And they also knew that Governor Franklin and his wife had generously donated a pulpit, desk, and

Old Saint Mary's Episcopal Church

145 West Broad Street
Burlington, NJ 08016
609-386-0902
www.stmarysburlington.org

NRIS 72000770
NHL

DATE BUILT
1703

SIGNIFICANCE
Old Saint Mary's Episcopal
Church has stood on the corner
of Wood and Broad Streets for
more than 300 years. During the
American Revolution it was the
scene of wrenching arguments
among its members, many of
whom, such as New Jersey's
royal governor William Franklin,
remained loyal to the English
king and refused to pay allegiance to the Continental
Congress that met across the
Delaware River in Philadelphia.

table when the greatly expanded church was completed
just seven years earlier in 1769. But now the question
went beyond the church's new refinements and even the
political commitment of their spiritual leader.

Complicating the situation was that fifteen miles
away, across the Delaware River, William Franklin's
father sat in the Continental Congress selecting a committee to meet with New Jersey's radical leaders and
counteract the obstructionism of his son. This man was
none other than Benjamin Franklin, idolized by many
for his civic contributions, scientific achievements, and
efforts in England to change the mother country's colonial policies. Samuel Adams, the Congressional delegate
from Massachusetts, John Jay, from New York, John
Dickinson, from Pennsylvania, and George Wythe, from
Virginia, were deputized to convince the New Jersey
legislature to resist its loyalist governor. Now Benjamin
Franklin and his son, William Franklin, who had occupied the royal governorship of New Jersey since 1762,
were at loggerheads. Nearly seventy, Benjamin was a
committed revolutionary; William, his forty-eight-year-
old son, was a committed servant of the English king.

Many in the congregation at St. Mary's had drifted
into the patriot ranks by early 1776, but many others,
like William Franklin and Odell, remained staunchly
loyalist, willing to suffer the consequences once
independence was declared. In public memory, the
Americans who remained loyal to England, which
necessarily meant opposing independence, would be
known as Tories, and the patriots were known as Whigs.
The Whigs painted their opponents as self-interested
conservatives protecting their status and wealth. This
image was bolstered by the fact that many loyalists were
British-appointed officials such as William Franklin,
wealthy citizens such as lawyers and merchants, and
people who simply feared the patriots' central vision
of an independent, redesigned United States whose
political, economic, and social power would be more
evenly distributed.

Behind these loyalist leaders stood thousands of
ordinary colonists, like many of St. Mary's members,
who refused to participate in the war for independence.
Representing at least one-fifth of the white population,
they fought against their former friends, community
members, and even family members, turning the

Revolutionary War into a civil war as well. British officers recruited thousands of colonists to fight for the king in provincial loyalist battalions with names such as the Loyalist New Jersey Volunteers and the Fourth Continental Dragoons. Deep into the war, some British strategists believed that they would have to Americanize the war, pressing into action the large reservoirs of armed loyalists. This was precisely what William Franklin pushed for, but for the most part the British military leaders decided against it.

By the first week of January 1776, William Franklin's grip on the New Jersey governorship was slipping away, which dismayed some St. Mary's worshipers but pleased others. Some militia officers who took communion at the church had already traded in their royal commissions for new appointments issued by New Jersey's assembly. Not a single newspaper circulated in New Jersey presented the loyalist point of view. Near and far, the suppression of Tory dissent had moved from intimidation and ostracism to tarring and feathering and other forms of physical abuse meant to wring pledges of allegiance to "the true sons of liberty" from the Tories. Nor could Governor Franklin convince the assembly not to listen to the delegation from the Continental Congress, sent to undermine his loyalist position. After listening to this delegation, New Jersey assemblymen voted against petitioning the king further and seeking a separate peace—actions that would have undermined the Continental Congress's attempt to define itself as the coordinator of all colonial protests.

On January 8, 1776, New Jersey's ranking revolutionary officer issued the order to arrest Governor Franklin. Held under house arrest, St. Mary's most important pew holder tried to send to England a letter promising, "Whatever may happen, I am determined that nothing shall influence me to swerve in the least from that loyalty and duty which I owe his Majesty, which has been the pride of my life." The next day, Thomas Paine's fiery *Common Sense* came off the press in Philadelphia. Governor Franklin lived under house arrest in Perth Amboy, New Jersey, where he had moved his governor's residence, for another five months. On June 25, the Second Continental Congress ordered Franklin taken to Connecticut and confined there. Undaunted to the end, he maintained his loyalty to the king. In a parting shot to the New Jersey radical legislators, Franklin wrote to the New Jersey legislature twelve days before the Declaration of Independence imploring them:

> to avoid, above all things, the traps of independency and republicanism now set before you, however tempting they may be baited. Depend upon it, you can never place yourselves in a happier situation than in your ancient constitutional dependency on Great Britain. No independent state ever was, or ever can be, so happy as we have been, and still might be, under that government.

Five months after Congress declared independence, New Jersey's revolutionary authorities arrested Jonathan Odell, who had been hiding in Franklin's riverfront mansion. Like most other Anglican ministers who had remained loyal to their king, Odell had to give up his church position. After being released, he took refuge with the British forces in New York, while leaving his wife and three children in Burlington, where they remained as hostages. But when the British occupied Philadelphia in the fall of 1777, Odell rejoined his family and accepted the appointment to be the press censor in charge of shutting down Philadelphia and Burlington's patriot newspapers. He left with the British when they evacuated the city in June 1778, going with them to New York.

St. Mary's most prominent figures continued to lead the loyalist cause, though they could no longer worship at the church. After being imprisoned in Connecticut for more than two years, William Franklin was released in November 1778 in exchange for the patriot governor of Delaware, whom the British had captured. Arriving in New York City, still the center of the British war administration, Franklin found himself among some 40,000 British soldiers and sailors and nearly 20,000 loyalist refugees who were formed into sixty-two companies of armed American loyalists. Unbending as before, he devoted himself completely to the loyalist cause. He persuaded General Henry Clinton to employ Jonathan Odell, St. Mary's refugee minister, as a propagandist. Odell filled the city's loyalist newspapers with satiric poems and stories that taunted the rebels and amused

A Conservative Lashes the Revolutionary Leaders

 Samuel Seabury, an Anglican minister in New York City, was an out-spoken critic of the American radical leadership urging independence. Anglicans were numerous among those who supported the king, and it is no coincidence that strongly Anglican New York was also heavily loyalist. Seabury's pungent prose, taken from one of his pamphlets, shows that his loyalty to the king was deeply tinctured by distrust of the democratic character of the radical revolutionists, who sought not only a war of independence but a more equal society.

Anarchy and confusion, violence and oppression, distress my country; and I must, and will speak. Though the open violator of the laws may escape punishment, through the pusillanimity of the magistrates, he shall feel the lash of my pen.... But perhaps you will say, that these men are contending for our rights; that they are defending our liberties; and though they act against the law, yet that the necessity of the times will justify them. Let me see. I sell a number of sheep. I drive them to New York, and deliver them to the purchaser. A mob interposes, and obliges me to take my sheep again, and drive them home for my pains, or sell them there for just what they please to give me. Are these the rights, is this the liberty, these men are contending for? It is vile, abject slavery, and I will have none of it. These men defend our rights, and liberties, who act in open defiance of the laws? No. They are making us the most abject slaves that ever existed. The necessity of the times justify them in violating the first principles of civil society! Who induced this necessity? Who involved the province in discord, anarchy and confusion? These very men. They created that necessity, which they now plead in their own justification.... If I must be enslaved, let it be by a King at least and not by a parcel of upstart lawless Committee-men. If I must be devoured, let me be devoured by the jaws of a lion, and not gnawed to death by rats and vermin.

A graduate of Yale, Samuel Seabury remained loyal to England and fled from his home in Connecticut to join the British troops occupying New York City. After the war, Connecticut leaders accepted him back into the fold.

the loyalist refugees. He also became involved in arranging Benedict Arnold's defection to the British in 1780.

At the war's end, Franklin sailed for London, where he spent the rest of his life. Odell was among 14,000 loyalists who constructed new lives in the Canadian province of New Brunswick. On a brief stay in London in 1783–84, where he had an audience with King George III, Odell found William Franklin acting as the chief lobbyist for the loyalists in their attempt to get some compensation from Parliament for their confiscated American estates.

Today a part of the Burlington Historic District, St. Mary's is one of New Jersey's oldest standing churches. St. Mary's has gone through many changes in its three centuries of existence. Refurbished in 1769, it was nearly tripled in size from its original thirty-three-foot by twenty-two-foot dimensions and graced with a new belfry. The church's chaste interior and its uncushioned pews reflected the modest status of most of its original members—shopkeepers, ship captains, small merchants, and artisans—in a riverside town of only several thousand inhabitants. The brick church stands on the corner of Wood and Broad Streets, just a few blocks from the

Delaware River. It was only a short distance from the handsome three-story brick house that William and Elizabeth Franklin built in the 1760s.

It took time to heal the wounds from the revolutionary era, but slowly the church, under a new minister, rebuilt its congregation. In 1810–11, South Carolina architect Robert Mills designed a five-sided apse that was added to the east end of the church. A generation later, in 1834–35, Isaac Holden of Philadelphia designed two additions to accommodate the growing parish, giving the formerly rectangular building a cruciform shape. The exterior brick was stuccoed over to provide a uniform appearance. In 1854, Burlington's Episcopalians built a new St. Mary's Church, but Old St. Mary's served as a parish Sunday school. When a fire destroyed much of the interior of the new St. Mary's in 1976, the old church was again used for worship for three years. The restoration of Old St. Mary's began in late 1999 and will be completed in time to celebrate the venerable building's 300th anniversary in 2003.

QUAKER MEETING HOUSE AND SCHOOL

340 High Street
Burlington, NJ 08016
609-387-3875
NHR

The Society of Friends (Quaker) meeting-house, standing on tree-lined High Street in Burlington, New Jersey, was built just after the American Revolution to replace the much smaller place of worship completed in 1687 by the founding Quakers of the New Jersey town on the Delaware River. From its beginnings in 1682, Burlington remained strongly Quaker. In keeping with the Quaker belief in the ability of each individual to find a personal connection with God without benefit of a trained minister, the meeting house had no pulpit, no ornamentation, and no organ or choir stalls. Two-and-a-half stories high, the brick meetinghouse is enclosed by a brick wall. In keeping with the Quakers' desire for simplicity and absence of ostentation, the meetinghouse has two plain entrances and simple sash windows.

The Quaker Meeting House became the site of much anguish during the American Revolution. Like Quakers elsewhere, Burlington's Friends were maligned as loyalists because most of them criticized American resistance to Great Britain, condemned organized boycotts of imported British goods, and became afraid of mass meetings and radical Whig street politics involving artisans and shopkeepers. They firmly believed that they owed allegiance to George III, the English king, because his royal predecessors had provided and protected religious liberties since the founding of Pennsylvania and New Jersey. When resistance to British policies turned into war in 1775, most Quakers disavowed the patriot movement on both pacifist and political grounds and disowned Quakers who participated in any activities that defied royal authority or led to combat.

Some patriot leaders sympathized with and respected the Quakers' "peace testimony," an absolute refusal to bear arms or engage in any violent acts. But most patriots suspected the wealthy Quakers were more interested in protecting their property than their principles. This situation became nearly untenable for the Quakers as the Revolution approached.

Especially offensive to the patriots was that while Quakers were exempted from military service, they refused to pay non-Quaker substitutes to serve for them or even to pay penalties for not serving, money that would support the families of those who were shedding their blood for the American cause. In the end, a number of Burlington Quakers left the Society of Friends to fight on the American side, but most refused to swear oaths disavowing the king and supporting the new state constitution.

The revolutionary experience of Margaret Hill Morris, a Quaker woman who worshiped at the Wood Street Meeting House, reveals the fine line most Quakers tried to straddle. In early December 1776, hearing that British forces were approaching Burlington, the widow Morris and her sister decided to remain in their house. When the British left, the patriots returned to search for loyalists. Morris hid loyalist minister Jonathan Odell in an attic room, diverted the patriots to another house, and later hustled him to another safe house from which he escaped to New York. That night, she warned another young man in Burlington that he was about to be seized as a Tory.

Yet Morris also helped patriot soldiers. When they were in the Burlington region, she sheltered them in her house, baked pies for them, tended their fires, and bound their wounds. Pacifist to the core and thoroughly humanitarian, she typified thousands of Quakers who thought the patriot call to arms was sinful and ill-advised but nonetheless rendered humanitarian services to the casualties of war.

ISAAC ROYALL HOUSE

15 George Street
Medford, MA 02153
NHL

Like William Franklin, Isaac Royall, Jr., remained loyal to his English king and paid the same price as Franklin—a life of exile in England. Living in Medford, five miles from Boston, he served on the council of the Massachusetts royal governor for twenty-two years. Frightened by radicals such as Sam Adams and Paul Revere,

The stately Royall House was used before the Civil War as a stop on the Underground Railroad—an ironic twist considering that this mansion is the only one in the North that still has slave quarters attached.

he joined the British after they occupied Boston in 1775 and left with them when George Washington drove the British out of the city. Royall fled to Halifax, Nova Scotia, and then took his family to London, where he died of smallpox in 1781.

Royall's mansion in Medford, situated along the Mystic River, started out as a modest brick house, built in 1637 by John Winthrop, the first governor of Massachusetts. It was only one room deep and two-and-a-half stories high; but went through many enlargements and renovations over the years, the first when Lieutenant Governor John Usher acquired it in 1697. The house was remodeled again between 1733 and 1737 by Isaac Royall, Sr., who arrived as a wealthy merchant from Antigua. Enlarged to include three stories, the house now acquired ornate interior decorations. It was also fitted out with slave quarters attached to the house for the twenty-seven slaves Royall brought from the West Indies. After inheriting the house from his father in 1739, Isaac Royall, Jr., renovated it again between 1747 and 1750, making it into a stately mansion with five large windows on each floor, a gabled roof, and an elaborate central doorway.

KINGS MOUNTAIN NATIONAL MILITARY PARK

Blacksburg, SC 29702
864-936-7921
www.nps.gov/kimo
NPS

The nearly 4,000 acres of Kings Mountain National Military Park lie just inside the northern border of South Carolina in the gently rolling Piedmont region. It was here that

American loyalists and patriots from North and South Carolina fought a bitter battle on October 7, 1780. This battle broke the back of strong loyalist sentiment in the South and became an important stepping-stone to the British surrender at Yorktown twelve months later. Although Kings Mountain is celebrated as a victory of volunteer militiamen from the mountain valleys of the western Carolinas, the enemy was not red-coated British soldiers but fellow colonists organized into a loyalist militia. Of the several thousand who fought at Kings Mountain in October 1780, every combatant but one was an American. A professional British soldier, Major Patrick Ferguson commanded the loyalist militia, but those fighting under him were colonial settlers, some of them related to those they fought against.

State and national attention to the pivotal battle came very slowly. As early as 1815 a small marker was erected on the battlefield, but it was not until a century after the battle, in 1880, that serious notice was paid to making the site a part of the public's memory of the American Revolution. In this year, private and state subscriptions led to the purchase of forty acres at the battle site, where a centennial monument was erected. Another twenty-nine years passed before Congress appropriated funds for a U.S. monument, which would be designed by the distinguished New York architectural firm of McKim, Mead, and White. In the early twentieth century, local chapters of the Daughters of the American Revolution placed a number of historical battleground markers at the site.

Reflecting the growing interest in commemorating Revolutionary War battle sites, 75,000 persons turned out in 1930, on the 150th anniversary of the battle, to hear President Herbert Hoover extol the heroism of the patriot militia. The next year, Congress established the Kings Mountain National Military Park. The National Park Service assumed direction of the park in 1933. From 1937 to 1942, Civilian Conservation Corps workers developed a reenactment area and constructed the battleground walking tours that visitors enjoy today.

Old South Meeting House

Boston, Mass.

Religion and Revolution

The Old South Meeting House was not only Boston's largest church but also the largest building in the city at the time of the American Revolution. At revolutionary-era mass meetings, Bostonians crowded through the windows when the door was jammed with citizens.

On Sundays, week after week, Bostonians entered the Old South Meeting House silently and reverently. But on the evening of Thursday, December 16, 1773, they crowded into the old Puritan house of worship irreverently and in full cry. A total of 5,000 men—nearly every man in the town—packed the church to protest the British tax on tea. After hours of stormy debate, Samuel Adams cried out in carefully coded words, "This meeting can do nothing more to save the country!" With that, the crowd stormed out of Old South and surged toward Griffin's Wharf several hundred yards away. Some of them, dressed as Native Americans and with faces blackened, leaped into action, dumping three shiploads of tea into Boston Harbor. From Old South, the city's largest spiritual sanctuary, the road to revolution had been paved.

For Boston loyalist Peter Oliver, the city's patriot Puritan clergymen were "Mr. Otis's Black Regiment," who preached sedition from their pulpits instead of warding off sin. Lord Hugh Percy, the adjutant of British General George Gage, agreed: "No body of men in the Province," he wrote in 1774, "are so extremely injurious to the peace and tranquility of it as the clergy. They preach up sedition openly from their pulpits." It was hardly true that lawyer James Otis, the fiery patriot leader, controlled the town's many clergymen. But Oliver and Lord Percy were right that by the 1770s, with the exception of Boston's Anglican minister, Henry Caner, and several other clergymen, the city's religious leaders had abandoned the political neutrality that ministers were supposed to observe. Revolution and religion became entwined, not only in Boston but in hundreds of other colonial communities.

Boston's Old South Meeting House, at the corner of Washington and Milk Streets, is the most memorable of the many buildings where religion and politics mixed during the American Revolution. Walking through the church today, visitors can gaze at the handsome raised pulpit and graceful galleries and imagine how Old South became Boston's premier site of protest, a place where the pulpit was as much a lectern for excoriating British policies as a platform for delivering sermons. Just as American churches became sites for organizing against discrimination and segregation in the civil rights movement of the 1960s, Old South served as both religious sanctuary and political forum in the advent of the American Revolution.

Old South Meeting House was erected in 1729 to replace its predecessor, a church built in 1669 which could no longer accommodate the growing Puritan congregation. One of its members, Richard Grant White, recalled Old South as "the perfect model of a New England 'meeting-house' of the highest style in the olden time." Its octagonal spire was the pride of the church's worshipers. If the gracious, elegant spire inspired awe, Old South's bare interior held to the old tradition of the Puritan meeting house "the hard, utilitarian, unsentimental spirit of the old New England life . . . no charm of color, . . . no grace of form . . . no monuments of departed notability. . . to divert the eye and mind from religious business."

Old South became almost an extension of Faneuil Hall, where "the body of the people" could assemble to demand their rights. Minister Joseph Sewall and his successors at Old South, dressed in black clerical garb, gave sermons on Sundays and held to the rule that the pulpit was above politics. But on Saturdays, plain-dressed Sam Adams, Thomas Hancock, and Dr. Joseph Warren, leaders of Boston's resistance to British policies, stood in the pulpit to address huge crowds of Bostonians who were not, for the most part, members of Old South's congregation. Whenever the crowd overwhelmed Faneuil Hall's capacity of 1,200 (as it frequently did), the town hall moderator called for reconvening the assembly in Old South, and the throng would quickly troop through the narrow streets for a few blocks until they reached the meetinghouse. Here 5,000 people or more could pack the pews, galleries, and aisles.

Old South Meeting House

310 Washington Street
Boston, MA 02108
617-482-6439
www.oldsouthmeetinghouse.org
www.nps.gov/bost

NRIS 66000778
NHL/NPS

DATE BUILT
1729

ORIGINAL OWNER
Members of the church

SIGNIFICANCE
Many of the most important protests against British policies in the 1760s and 1770s took place here in the North End of the city. Although its congregation moved west to the Back Bay area in the nineteenth century, Old South remained a venue for spirited debates and has been preserved as a historic shrine.

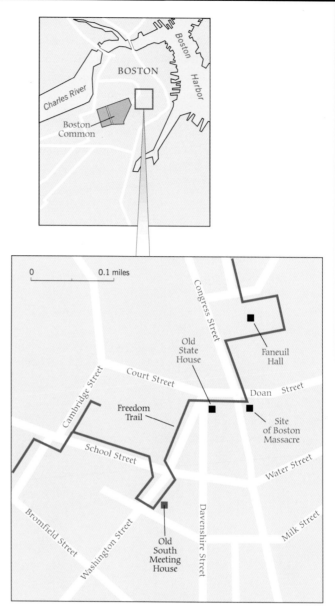

The first use of Old South as the site of an overflow town meeting occurred on June 14, 1768, when Bostonians assembled to protest the seizure of John Hancock's ship the *Liberty,* which had been smuggling goods into the town without paying custom duties. James Otis gave an impassioned political sermon from Old South's pulpit—the first step in braiding together religion and politics. "The grievances the people labor under may in time be removed; if not," he proclaimed prophetically, "and we are called on to defend our liberty and privileges, I hope, and believe we shall, one and all, resist unto blood." And twenty-one months later, the day after the Boston Massacre on March 5, 1770, Bostonians of all ranks swamped Old South to decide what to do about their bloodstained cobblestones.

March 5 became an occasion every year for orators to perpetuate the memory of the six martyrs who died in the massacre and to keep the fires of resistance to the British burning brightly. At dusk on December 16, 1773, the overflow crowd at Faneuil Hall poured into Old South to hear Sam Adams's ominous words "This meeting can do nothing further to save the country." This was the signal for painted "Mohawks" in the galleries and in the street outside to head for the waterfront, where they boarded three British ships with 342 chests of India tea and dumped all the tea into the harbor.

Old South reverberated again three months later, on March 5, 1774 (called Massacre Day to honor the Boston Massacre victims), when John Hancock delivered sledgehammer blows against the British. Sam and John Adams were among the patriot leaders present, and Sam Adams wrote of the "spirited performance" and the "vast crowd" with "rainy eyes." "I conjure you by all that is dear," Hancock exhorted his listeners, "by all that is honourable, by all that is sacred, not only that ye pray, but that you act; that if necessary ye fight and even die for the prosperity of our Jerusalem. Break asunder, with noble disdain, the bonds with which the Philistines have bound you." For the Massacre Day oration the next year, when some forty British officers were in Old South, Joseph Warren had to climb in a window to get to the pulpit because the church floor was so packed. The red-coated officers had little effect on moderating Warren's oration. "The American beholds the Briton as the Russian, ready *first* to take away his property, and *next* what is dearer to every virtuous man, the liberty of his country," he proclaimed. Outside the church, the British 47th Regiment marched by with drums beating to drown out Warren's incendiary address.

Just as merchants and doctors such as Hancock and Warren peppered their speeches with biblical allusions, so did Boston's clergymen orate in political terms as the line between secular and sacred disappeared. Samuel Cooper, minister at wealthy Brattle Street Church and nephew of Old South's minister, Joseph Sewall, was at the center of the Boston revolutionary movement. The eighty-year-old Sewall, in the fifty-fifth year of his pastorate by

1768, was more reticent, protecting the cherished idea that the sacred calling permitted no mingling in politics. But he freely gave up his church to mass political meetings and privately supported the cause of resisting what most of his congregation believed to be a war to protect their hard-earned liberties.

The reverse was true at Brattle Street Church. Boston's citizens never gathered here for political meetings, but the man who stood in the pulpit every Sunday spent much of the other six days operating covertly at the center of revolutionary politics. From the Stamp Act crisis in 1765 to the closing of Boston's port by the Coercive Act of 1774, Cooper was careful not to preach politics from the pulpit for fear of dividing his congregation, which included many supporters of royal government in Massachusetts. But thereafter, with only a few in his congregation remaining unconverted to the resistance movement, he discarded the political neutrality of his pulpit.

This propaganda piece engraved by Paul Revere shows a British officer on the right waving his sword to release a deadly volley against what appear to be innocent Bostonians. In reality, the Boston mob was harassing the soldiers, and a British officer tried to prevent bloodshed. Copied widely in Europe as well as in the colonies, the picture fueled support for the colonists against the British.

Revolutionary Oratory in Old South Meeting House

Every year after the Boston Massacre, Bostonians gathered in Old South Meeting House on March 5 or 6 (if the fifth fell on a Sunday) to commemorate the Bostonians who died in the snow-covered street in 1770. In 1775, Dr. Joseph Warren gave the oration before the packed church. These passages from his oration show how the house of worship was used to call Bostonians to arms.

On you depend the fortunes of America. You are to decide the important question, on which rest the happiness and liberty of millions yet unborn. Act worthy or yourselves. The faltering tongue of hoary age calls on you to support your country. ...I mourn over my bleeding country: ...You the, who nobly espoused your Country's cause, who generously have sacrificed wealth and ease, who have despised the pomp and show of tinsel'd greatness...who have forsaken the downy pillow, to keep your vigils by the midnight lamp, for the salvation of your invaded country...you will then reap that harvest of renown which you so justly have deserved. Your country shall pay her grateful tribute of applause. Even the children of your most inveterate enemies, ashamed to tell from whom they sprang, while they in secret curse their stupid, cruel parents, shall join the general voice of gratitude to those who broke the fetters which their fathers forged.

Nine days after Warren's Old South oration, Boston Tories (those opposed to the radical revolutionaries) met at the British Coffee House to listen to a scorching ridicule of the revolutionary leaders by Dr. Thomas Bolton. Like Warren's oration, this address was quickly published in a pamphlet.

I cannot boast the ignorance of [John] Hancock, the insolence of [Samuel] Adams, the absurdity of [John] Rowe [a merchant],...the turgid bombast of [Joseph] Warren, the treasons of [Josiah] Quincy, the hypocrisy of [William] Cooper [Boston's town clerk], nor the principles of [Thomas] Young....With regard to their political schemes, I challenge all Hell to match them....

A Whig my dear friends is a notable thing,
We can trample on justice, and rail at
    the king.
We can laugh at religion, nor ne'er care a fig
For law or for gospel. This is a true Whig.

Old South and other Boston churches involved in radical politics suffered greatly after British regiments turned the city into their garrison in April 1775. While patriots fled the city, the occupying army took its revenge on "the ministers of sedition." They particularly targeted "dissenting chapels," the term used by British soldiers raised in Church of England doctrine to describe the Puritan Presbyterian and Congregational churches.

Old South Meeting House, along with the house of Sam Adams, was singled out for special abuse. The pulpit and all the pews were torn up and converted into firewood. The parsonage and sycamores in front of the church suffered the same fate. The ornately carved pew of Deacon Thomas Hubbard was carried off and turned into a pigsty. In order to convert the church into a horse-riding ring, the British soldiers covered the floor with several hundred loads of gravel, dirt, and tanbark. Here the Queen's Light Dragoons schooled their mounts, as wives and guests watched the horsemanship from the east gallery while sipping alcoholic refreshments from a bar fitted out for these occasions. Many other churches suffered similar degradations. Old North Church was completely razed to keep the British warm under the military axiom that "the King must have wood." Occupying British troops tore down the steeple of West Church in 1775 to prevent its being used to send signals to revolutionaries across the Back Bay.

After the British withdrew from Boston in March 1776, Old South's congregation began the laborious work of restoring their church and putting its finances on a firm footing. Yet after the war, the edifice retained the dual personality it had acquired in the tumultuous 1770s as a place of worship and a venue for political commemorations. Old South became the site of July Fourth prayers, choruses, and thumping orations. In the 1840s, remembering that Old South was Phillis Wheatley's church, the congregation was caught up in the abolitionist fervor.

When the meetinghouse was about to be put on the auction block for salvage in 1875, it was fitting that Wendell Phillips, one of Boston's most eloquent orators, insisted that Bostonians were about to throw away both a sacred building and a key link to the history of the American Revolution. Here was where revolutionary crowds gathered to hear the eloquence of Otis, Sam

Adams, Hancock, and Warren. Here was the last building still standing in the neighborhood of the famous events of the 1770s, "just below where [Crispus] Attucks fell (our first martyr [killed in the Boston Massacre]), and just above where zealous patriots made a teapot of the harbor." "What does *Boston* mean?" asked Phillips. "Since 1630 the living fibre running through history which owns the name [Boston] means jealousy of power, unfettered speech, keen sense of justice, readiness to champion any good cause. That is the Boston [Archbishop] Laud suspected, [Lord] North hated, and the Negro loved."

Old South was nearly lost again to the wrecker's ball in 1872 after its congregation followed the congregations of other venerable churches to the Back Bay, where they built more fashionable churches of stone rather than brick or wood. In this case, the descendants of Old South's Revolutionary War parishioners built a Gothic church with an impressive campanile (bell tower). With the church scheduled for demolition, a group of Bostonians formed the Old South Association in 1876 and raised $400,000 to rescue the venerable church as a historic monument. For the first time in

This detail of a 1769 map of Boston shows the narrow and crooked streets of the city's North End.

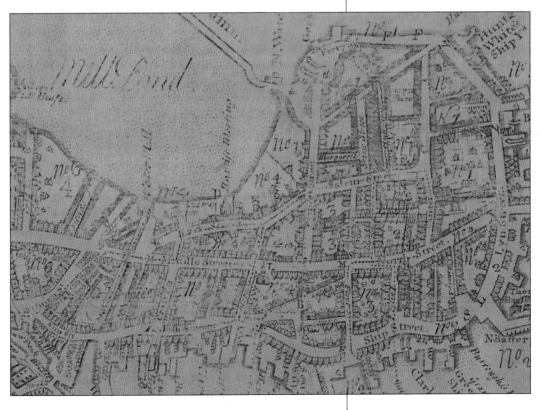

Boston, citizens determined to respect the city's historical and architectural heritage triumphed over the relentless urge to modernize the city and obliterate important historic sites when profit and expediency beckoned.

After Old South became a historical monument in 1876, the Old South Association tried to distance itself from the building's radical past. But this led to controversy and spirited public debate. Boston Brahmins (members of the city's upper-class, old-family community) on the association's board wanted it to be a patriotic shrine where ancestral history groups could hold their meetings and not "made a place for preaching socialistic or pacifistic doctrines," as Charles Eliot, president of the Old South Association and president emeritus of Harvard University, argued in 1918. But younger members of the association, seeing Old South as a monument to free speech and free assembly, argued differently. By the late 1920s, the Old South Association was caught up in controversy over allowing a group to memorialize Nicola Sacco and Bartolomeo Vanzetti, who had been executed in 1927 for murder on what many believed were trumped-up charges meant to get rid of two admitted anarchists. The association relented after much discussion about the church's historic free speech role during the American Revolution.

In 1951 Old South became a key feature of the Freedom Trail, a self-guided walking tour that turned into a major tourist attraction. The building itself became part of the National Park Service's Boston National Historical Park in 1974. Today, Old South is still a place for groups to assemble, a symbol of free speech, and a center of educational activities.

A Church's Rebirth as Historic Site

Like almost every American church, Christ Church suffered physical blows in the nineteenth and early twentieth centuries—fire, water damage, and structural rot. But what threatened the church even more was the flight of its congregation to the suburbs. Rising in Philadelphia's colonial commercial center two blocks from the Delaware River waterfront, it stood at the beginning of the twentieth century in a densely packed neighborhood of poor immigrants. On the eve of World War I, a Philadelphia newspaper claimed that Christ Church was "regarded by the general public simply as an historic shrine to be visited by the curious or patriotic pilgrim to our city" rather than as a functioning church. It took much time, considerable controversy, and finally a crusading, progressive rector, Louis Cope Washburn, to reinvent Christ Church as an urban church serving the downtrodden people of its parish while preserving the edifice as a historic shrine.

Christ Church's historic importance was enhanced by its designation as a national site in 1947, two years after its 250th anniversary. This congressional decision carried with it governmental stewardship of the building. Two years later, the church became part of the newly created Independence National Historic Park. Protecting the church from fire was an important goal, and this was achieved by acquiring adjacent property with run-down buildings and demolishing them to create parklike surroundings. By the 1950s, the church was losing its congregation and its financial underpinning. But by calling itself "the Nation's church" and promoting its historical importance, Christ Church became a key part of showcasing Philadelphia's history.

NASSAU HALL

Princeton University
Princeton, NJ 08544
609-258-6115
NHL

Erected between 1754 and 1756, Nassau Hall housed the College of New Jersey, which later became Princeton University. Dominated by Presbyterians it was the most important college building in the mid-Atlantic colonies. Its elegant design influenced the architecture of other colleges in succeeding decades. During the American Revolution, it became a place where religion and politics were fused when the college's president, John Witherspoon, became a patriot preacher and politician as well as an educator. The College of New Jersey had recruited the Scottish clergyman in 1768, and it did not take long for him to embrace the American cause. Formally, he respected the Presbyterian synod's position that the pulpit should never become a political platform. But by 1775 Witherspoon not only began to preach politics, but he became a politician, accepting the chairmanship of the local Committee of Correspondence. Within another year he was elected a member of the New Jersey congress and then became one of New Jersey's four delegates to the Second Continental Congress, where he signed the Declaration of Independence.

Architects from the Carpenter's Company of Philadelphia were imported to design and supervise construction of the plain three-story Georgian-style building. Using brownstone dug from a local quarry, Robert Smith and William Shippen planned a 177-foot-long structure that served as dormitory, dining hall, chapel, classroom, and library. After Nassau Hall was completed, seventy students enrolled in the college, and this was about the number of students studying there when the Revolutionary War broke out. Nassau Hall suffered all the indignities perpetrated by an occupying British army, which left the village and college in ruins in December 1776. Taking stock after the British departure, the Philadelphia doctor Benjamin Rush reported: "You would think it had been desolated with the plague and earthquake, as well as . . . war; the college and church are heaps of ruin; all the inhabitants have been plundered."

The fusion of religion, education, and politics continued at Nassau Hall throughout the Revolution. After declaring independence, New Jersey's delegates drew up the state's first constitution in the building. The first New Jersey governor under the new constitution, William Livingston, was inaugurated here as well. During the war, the Continental Army used the building for a commissary, a hospital, and a prison for captured British soldiers and loyalists. In the summer and fall of 1783, the Continental Congress—harried out of Philadelphia by mutinous troops demanding back pay—convened in Nassau Hall where they welcomed the first emissary to the new nation from abroad, the Minister of the Netherlands.

Nassau Hall suffered repeatedly in the nineteenth century. In 1802, a fire left only the walls standing. It was reconstructed by the noted architect Benjamin Latrobe, who also restored the unfinished U.S. Capitol building in Washington, D.C., after it was burned by the British in 1814. After another fire in 1855, a third reconstruction in 1860 provided Nassau Hall with a Florentine-style central doorway was added, as well as a much higher cupola that gave the building an additional Renaissance touch.

The venerable building underwent many interior renovations in subsequent decades, but its external appearance today is unchanged from the reconstruction completed in 1860. In 1896 the College of New Jersey became Princeton University. In 1961 Nassau Hall was designated a National Historical Landmark.

TOURO SYNAGOGUE

72 Touro Street
Newport, RI 02840
401-847-4794
www.tourosynagogue.org
www.nps.gov/tosy
NPS

The American Revolution not only involved churches with divided congregations but in some cases nearly destroyed them. One of these was the congregation of Touro Synagogue. Built by Sephardic Jews, mostly of Portuguese and Spanish origin, who had arrived in the mid-

Women and men worship separately in some Jewish synagogues. The women's gallery is above the sanctuary floor in Touro Synagogue, the only surviving synagogue building from the colonial period.

eighteenth century, the synagogue was led by Rabbi Isaac Touro. With funds gathered from many sources, these Jews commissioned Peter Harrison, New England's most accomplished architect, to build the synagogue. It was dedicated in 1763, just as the Seven Years War ended.

Harrison's design was Georgian in style but unusual in the way it was angled toward the street so that the sanctuary's Holy Ark would face eastward toward Jerusalem. The exterior featured walls made of brick imported from England, Ionic columns, and arched Palladian windows. The interior resembled that of Spanish and Portuguese colonial synagogues; twelve Ionic columns, representing the twelve tribes of Israel, support a women's gallery. Surmounting them are twelve Corinthian columns holding up the domed ceiling. Each column was shaped from a solid tree trunk. The Holy Ark contained the scrolls of the Torah with silver-adorned wooden rollers designed by a Jewish silversmith.

The Revolution scattered Touro Synagogue's congregation, and it was not until 1883 that it reopened for religious use. It took another decade for a congregation to organize. In 1946 the synagogue was designated a National Historical Site, recognition of its status as the oldest standing synagogue in the United States.

In 1954 a newly organized Society of Friends of Touro Synagogue began extensive restoration of the buildings.

CHRIST CHURCH
Second Street, between Market and Arch Streets
Philadelphia, PA 19106
215-922-1695
www.christchurchphila.org
www.nps.gov/inde
NHL

Dominating Philadelphia's waterfront with its octagonal wooden spire rising to a height of 196 feet, Christ Church was the most ornate and imposing Anglican church in the colonies when war broke out in 1775. As in Boston's Old South Meeting House, politics and religion mingled, although few of its congregants wanted this to happen. But neither the ministers nor the congregants could possibly avoid the controversies that attended the onset of the American Revolution as the line between religion and politics blurred. Some of Philadelphia's revolutionary leaders, such as Benjamin Franklin, James Cannon, and Robert Morris, were pew holders, but so were many who welcomed the British occupation of Philadelphia in September 1777 and were later imprisoned as Tories.

Christ Church was constructed between 1727 and 1754, rising in Georgian style with an elegance unmatched at the time. Its massive Palladian window and twenty-eight-square-foot tower with stone walls four feet thick reflected the wealth and sophistication of its worshipers. A considerable number of Philadelphia's merchants and lawyers as well as prosperous carpenters, shipbuilders, silversmiths, clockmakers, and shopkeepers worshiped at Christ Church. Dr. John Kearsley, an amateur architect, is given credit for the church's design, but much recognition should go to the scores of Philadelphia construction artisans who trudged to Second Street for the twenty-seven years it took to complete the building. Atop the breathtaking spire was a royal crown. When lightning struck the crown in 1777—seen by many as a sign that God was on the American side—the church replaced it with a thirty-inch bishop's golden miter.

Francis Hopkinson House

Bordentown, N.J.

Arts and Arms

When General George Washington and his entourage entered Philadelphia on November 28, 1781, four weeks after accepting Lord Charles Cornwallis's surrender of about 8,300 British and Hessian troops at Yorktown, Virginia, he was greeted by a spectacular display of huge "transparencies"—paintings on varnished paper lit from behind by scores of lanterns. Created by Charles Willson Peale, the city's most famous artist, they showed huge pictures of Washington; a French warship menacing the British in Chesapeake Bay; and a Temple of Independence with thirteen columns surmounted by a pediment allegorically displaying Justice, Hope, Industry, and Brave Soldiery. "During the whole evening," wrote the *Pennsylvania Packet* newspaper "the people were flocking from all parts of the town to obtain a sight of the beautiful expressions of Mr. Peale's respect and gratitude to the conquering Hero."

Two weeks later, on December 11, 1781, Washington went to the Southwark Theater to see *The Temple of Minerva*, a play by Francis Hopkinson, a Philadelphia

Bordentown, New Jersey, where Francis Hopkinson's house stands, was a sleepy village. But its pulse quickened during the Revolution because of its proximity to Philadelphia.

lawyer and politician, that celebrated the American victory over the British, thanked France for its support, and hailed Washington. Here in the city where the Continental Congress had conducted the War of Independence, the arts—painting, music, poetry, and drama—made their contributions to the American cause.

It would be harder to mesh a life of literature, music, and art with business and politics more effectively than did Francis Hopkinson, who created most of his works in his spacious house in Bordentown, New Jersey. The first graduate of the College of Philadelphia (now the University of Pennsylvania) in 1757, Hopkinson was a well-established lawyer when the conflict between England and the American colonies began in the early 1760s. In 1774, William Franklin, New Jersey's royal governor, appointed him to his council, and two years later New Jersey's Assembly elected him as a delegate to the Second Continental Congress. In that role, he signed the Declaration of Independence.

Built in 1750 by merchant John Imlay, the Hopkinson House in Bordentown, a New Jersey village perched on a bluff above a great bend in the Delaware River, was Francis Hopkinson's home from 1768 to 1791. Hopkinson had married Ann Borden, whose father purchased the house from Imlay, and Hopkinson and Borden lived here after marrying in 1768. Built in an L-shape, the spacious three-story brick house boasts five rows of windows across the front, a center hall extending through the main part of the house (a typical feature of the period), a large living room on one side of the first floor, and a large library on the other side Hopkinson created his poems, ballads, and art in this library. The dining room and kitchen occupy the first-floor wing.

Frequently traveling the ten miles from his New Jersey home to Philadelphia—a half-day's ride by horse—Hopkinson served ably as a member of the Continental Congress's Navy Board, which oversaw naval matters during the Revolutionary War; as treasurer of loans from 1778 to 1781; and as judge of the Admiralty Court of Pennsylvania from 1779 to 1780. He also used his artistic abilities to further the American cause. Having already designed the seal of the University of Pennsylvania, he became the unofficial designer of seals and symbols for the emerging new nation. His

Francis Hopkinson House

101 Farnsworth Avenue
Bordentown, NJ 08505

NRIS 71000496
NHL

DATE BUILT
1750

ORIGINAL OWNER
John Imlay

SIGNIFICANCE
The Hopkinson House in Bordentown, New Jersey, was the home of one of the revolutionary era's political leaders, who also made large contributions to the American cause as an artist, poet, musician, and playwright.

drafting skills and artistic talents helped produce the designs for the seals of New Jersey, the Board of Admiralty, the Board of Treasury, and the Great Seal of the United States that is on the paper money we use today. Hopkinson's fame as an artist grew through his design of the first flag of the new United States: thirteen red and white alternating stripes and a circle of thirteen white stars on a blue field.

At his house in Bordentown, Hopkinson's multiple talents ranged from designer and draftsman to poet, musician, and political satirist. It is said that a song of his, "Beneath the Weeping Willow's Shade," was Washington's favorite. An accomplished organ and harpsichord player, he composed many musical pieces. Just before signing the Declaration of Independence, he produced *A Pretty Story,* a children's allegory about a family relationship gone sour. After the Revolution, he continued his artistic work, composing songs to be played on the piano and harpsichord and writing poems to celebrate the ratification of the Constitution in 1788.

When the British occupied Philadelphia in the winter of 1777–78, they plundered Hopkinson's nearby house. "These pot-valiant [filled with punch and wine] patriots sally forth and commit all manner of riot and excess in honour of their king and country," Hopkinson exclaimed. But this only inspired him to use art and literature to defeat the British. Mocking Sir William Howe's pleasant winter in occupied Philadelphia, where he made no move to attack Washington's suffering army at Valley Forge, Hopkinson's "Battle of the Kegs" became a popular ballad. It related how Bordentown's citizens floated kegs of gunpowder down the Delaware River in the hope that they would explode when reaching British warships anchored off Philadelphia's waterfront. The ballad also lampooned General Howe's amorous exploits:

> Awake, arouse, Sir Billy,
>
> There's forage in the plain,
>
> Ah, leave your little Filly,
>
> And open the Campaign
>
> Sir William he, snug as a flea,
>
> Lay all this time a snoring,
>
> Nor dream'd of harm as he lay warm,
>
> In bed with Mrs. L____g

Lift Every Voice

As in all wars, revolutions and social movements, song played a vital role in the American Revolution. "Indifferent songs," Pennsylvania's John Dickinson recognized, "are frequently very powerful on certain occasions." Boston's Sam Adams enthusiastically agreed and used his fine voice as a political instrument. Peter Oliver, one of Adams' Tory townsmen, accused him of "instituting singing societies of mechanicks [artisans], where he presided, and embraced such opportunities to the inculcating [of] sedition 'till it had ripened into rebellion." In 1768, when the arguments with England were fermenting, Philadelphia's John Dickinson penned a song, soon to be called "The Liberty Song," that became enormously popular and helped fuel the revolutionary movement. Printed in newspapers and broadsides, it was soon being sung by colonists everywhere: in the streets, in open fields, and at ritual celebrations such as Boston's commemoration of the Stamp Act Riot of August 14 and Charleston, South Carolina's dedication of a liberty tree. "This [song]," observed John Adams in his diary after coming home from a meeting of 350 Sons of Liberty, "is cultivating the sensations of freedom."

> COME join Hand in Hand, brave
> AMERICANS all,
> And rouse your bold Hearts at fair
> LIBERTY's Call;
> No *tyrannous Acts* shall suppress your
> just Claim,
> Or stain with *Dishonor* AMERICA's Name.
> Swarms of PLACEMEN and PENSIONERS
> soon will appear,
> Like Locusts deforming the Charms of
> the Year;
> Suns vainly will rise, Showers vainly
> descend,

> If we are to *drudge for* what *others shall*
> spend.
> In FREEDOM we're BORN, and in
> FREEDOM we'll LIVE,
> Our Purses are ready,
> Steady, Friends, Steady,
> Not as SLAVES, but as FREEMEN our
> Money we'll give.

"The Liberty Song" became the rallying cry of colonial resistance to the Townshend Revenue Acts of 1767 and continued to be sung down to the time of the Declaration of Independence and beyond. William Billings, a twenty-four-year-old tanner from Boston, could not fight in the American Revolution because he was blind in one eye and had a shortened leg and a withered arm that crippled him. But Billings served on the home front, becoming Boston's tune-smith, singing master, and promoter of musical and political harmony. In 1770, he published the New-England Psalm-Singer, the first collection of entirely American music, all of it written by Billings himself. Soon, noted Reverend William Bentley of Salem, this "self taught man had the direction of all the music of our churches." Over the years, Billings published 111 collections of music, much of it composed by New England singing masters like himself.

In 1770, he published a song that outdid even Dickinson's for patriotic appeal, at least in New England. In hundreds of churches and at secular meetings, patriots sang these lines from "Chester":

> Let tyrants shake their Iron rod
> And slav'ry Clank her galling Chains
> We fear them not we trust in god
> New England's god for ever reigns.

Mrs. Loring, Howe's "little filly," was a splashy blonde and the wife of Joshua Loring, the loyalist commissary of American prisoners in Philadelphia. As everyone knew, she was the British general's mistress.

Hopkinson, like many other American men of high culture, contributed to celebrate peace and independence through art, drama, and literature. "Peace, liberty, and independence," he wrote, would be "be-prosed and be-rhymed" and "set to every note in the scale of music" all over the country. Hopkinson did his best to make this happen with poems, essays, and musical tributes to the new nation.

After Hopkinson died in 1791, the house became the residence of his son Joseph, composer of the stirring anthem "Hail, Columbia." The house remained in the Hopkinson family until 1915, when it was purchased by a local judge. The exterior of the house is little altered from its mid-eighteenth-century appearance except for the roof. The interior retains its original center hall floor plan, but. much of the existing detailing was done in the early nineteenth century.

After writing the stirring "Liberty Song," John Dickinson became a reluctant revolutionist, afraid that the radicals in the vanguard of the movement for independence would push democratic reforms too far.

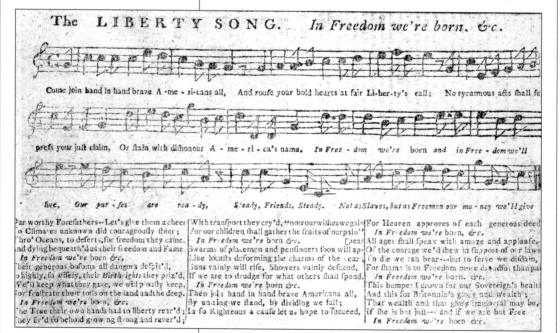

America's First Historical Museum

All the revolutionary generation's artistic energy found its focus through the inspiration of one of its finest exemplars, Charles Willson Peale. Consciously striving to be a public artist who would disseminate useful knowledge and keep the memory of the past before ordinary Americans, Peale created a museum in a skylighted addition to his Philadelphia home a year before the war ended. He planned this as a monument to American accomplishments. Peale filled his museum with natural history exhibits and some thirty paintings and wax figures of revolutionary heroes—Washington, Franklin, Paine, presidents of the Continental Congress, and many of Washington's generals. Peale moved his museum ten years later to Philosophical Hall, the home of the American Philosophical Society, a stone's throw from Independence Hall.

In 1802, when the federal government abandoned Independence Hall for Washington, D.C., Peale moved his rapidly growing museum into the place where the Declaration of Independence and the Constitution were signed. At this time, visitors were treated to 250 stuffed animals, including a grizzly bear, a buffalo, and a seven-foot anteater; several thousand birds in glass cases with painted backdrops appropriate to their natural environments; the first complete mastodon skeleton excavated in North America, which was twelve feet high and nineteen feet long; marine exhibits of mounted fish, amphibious specimens, and seashells; scientific experiments; some 4,000 insects and fossils; and a collection of paintings by Peale and his son Rembrandt.

Peale came close to realizing his dream of establishing a national science and art museum, but he fell short, ironically because the Jeffersonian political ideology that he enthusiastically espoused wanted to put strict limits on the areas where the government should intervene. This made state or federal support of his museum impossible. After his death in 1827, his fabulous collection was dispersed piecemeal. Much of it was sold to P. T. Barnum, who incorporated it in his American Museum in New York City in 1840; some of it was lost to fire. Many of his portraits of revolutionary heroes, however, did end up in his museum in Independence Hall. In time, it became a national portrait gallery.

Charles Willson Peale, the Revolutionary era's most prolific portrait painter, depicts himself drawing back a velvet curtain to show a mastodon skeleton excavated in Ulster County, New York. The mastodon was the star attraction of Peale's natural history museum, located in the upper floor of Independence Hall. At the top of the far wall are Peale's portraits of Revolutionary War heroes. Peale's Museum and Great School of Nature, as he called it, remained in Independence Hall until 1827.

PHILOSOPHICAL HALL

104 South Fifth Street
Philadelphia, PA 19106
215-440-3400
www.amphilsoc.org
NHL

Charles Willson Peale, the most gifted portrait painter of the revolutionary era, often hosted Francis Hopkinson, his comrade both in arms and in art, at his house on Lombard Street in Philadelphia. But Peale's house has not survived, and we can appreciate his extraordinary talent only through gazing at Philosophical Hall, just around the corner from Independence Hall in Philadelphia. Although planned as the home of the American Philosophical Society before the Revolution, construction did not begin until 1785 and was not completed for another four years. Two-and-a-half stories high, the handsome brick building has gabled dormers facing both east and west. Reserving only two rooms for its meetings, the Philosophical Society rented the rest of the building to Peale in 1794, and here he lived with his large family, his menagerie of exotic, caged birds and animals (with tame ones grazing in the State House Yard), and a bald eagle that roosted in a cage atop the building. Inside, visitors gazed at his Revolution-era portraits and thousands of natural history objects that he hoped he could turn into a national museum.

When Peale moved from Maryland to Philadelphia in 1775, he joined a militia company whose volunteers elected him an officer. Attached to Washington's tattered army, which was encamped across the Delaware River from the Hessians occupying Trenton in December 1776, Peale did guard duty by day and by night painted miniatures of officers and made them false teeth and fashioned rawhide moccasins for his noncommissioned men. It was a pattern of arms, craftsmanship, and art that occupied Peale for the remainder of the war. Well connected in radical circles, he became part of a group of artists and writers who propagandized for the American cause and used art and literature as political tools to forge consensus and lift spirits in the dark days of the war.

At Valley Forge in the winter of 1777–78, Peale continued his double role as soldier and artist. He carved little portraits in ivory for about forty officers, including Benedict Arnold, and began what became for him a minor industry painting likenesses of Washington. Mattress ticking had to serve for his first portrait because canvas was unavailable. The enterprising Peale, always struggling to support his growing family, made copies to sell to officers. After Peale returned to Philadelphia in June 1778, he created new portraits of Washington, and in 1779, the Pennsylvania revolutionary government commissioned him to paint Washington again. More likenesses of Washington would follow.

Often working with Hopkinson, Peale became Philadelphia's leading public artist, using art for expressly political purposes. It was Peale who painted the double-faced effigy of the turncoat Benedict Arnold that was paraded on a cart through Philadelphia and then burned in a ritualistic reviling of Arnold's treason in 1780. When Congress ratified the Treaty of Paris, officially ending the war in January 1783, Peale won the commission to deck the city out for a proper celebration. With a ($600 outlay (around $50,000 today), Peale produced a fifty-foot-wide triumphal arch constructed of wood, plaster, and paper painted to look like masonry across Market Street that was worthy of imperial Rome. In addition, 1,200 lamps inside the arches illuminated transparencies depicting Revolutionary War scenes, all handsomely inscribed with Latin mottoes, such as "By divine favor, a great and new order of the ages commences."

CHARLES WILLSON PEALE HOUSE ("BELFIELD")

2100 Clarkson Avenue
Philadelphia, PA 19144
NHL

In 1810, Charles Willson Peale moved from central Philadelphia to a hilltop house in North Philadelphia in search of rural serenity. Originally built in 1708 on a 104-acre piece of land, Peale intended this home to be both a place of repose and a place to experiment with horticulture and farming. While living in the house for 10 years, Peale made changes to transform it into a working studio and a repository for his voluminous historical materials and his endless projects. He also changed its name from "Farm Persevere," which perfectly expressed his approach to life, to "Belfield" after the name of his first mentor's estate in Maryland.

Belfield was sold in 1826 to William Logan Fisher, a wealthy Philadelphia Quaker. In the 19th century, his descendants added a third story to the house. In about 1900, a gambrel roof was added. Over the years, the 104 acres that had Peale purchased were reduced through subdivision and sale to 8 acres. Much of the farm became the Belfield Country Club, where golfers, tennis players, and cricketers played their games, most likely unaware that they were on the grounds farmed by the Revolution's most prolific artist. In 1984, La Salle University purchased Belfield and what was left of its acreage from descendants of the Fisher family. It is now the president's house at La Salle.

BENJAMIN WEST BIRTHPLACE

Swarthmore College campus
Swarthmore, PA 19081
610-328-8000
www.swarthmore.edu
NHL

Benjamin West, the teacher of the revolutionary generation's most gifted artists, including Gilbert Stuart, John Trumbull, Charles Willson Peale, and Thomas Sully, was born in the farmhouse that still stands on the campus of Swarthmore College. The house was constructed in 1724 of stone, with a gambrel roof, two dormers on the front, and two brick chimneys. These exterior features remain today, although the interior was completely reconstructed after a fire in 1874 gutted the building. The one-story extension at the north end of the house was added after 1874. The house is now a college faculty residence.

West had gone to England in 1763 to study painting and never returned to the colonies. But he supported American independence and planned a set of paintings on the American Revolution. They were later engraved and widely circulated in the new United States. Even from his perch in London, he had a major influence on the art of the American Revolution by training most of its most accomplished artists.

GOVERNOR JONATHAN TRUMBULL HOUSE

169 West Town Street
Lebanon, CT 06249
860-642-7558
NHL

The Governor Jonathan Trumbull House was the birthplace of Trumbull's son John, who gained fame as the foremost painter of Revolutionary War battle scenes and political conventions. Little altered over two and a half centuries, the Georgian-style house has a steep gable roof and a large central chimney. The central hall and stairway (typical of the period) bisect the parlor and dining room. Upstairs, the house was altered during the war to create a secret office for Governor Trumbull. In about 1830, the house was moved a short distance from its original site to the southwest corner of Lebanon Common. The house was purchased by the Daughters of the American Revolution in 1934 and was restored in the 1960s. It has original Trumbull furniture and an impressive pewter collection.

Born in this house in 1756, Connecticut artist John Trumbull sketched many revolutionary battle scenes from first-hand experience.

John Trumbull was a nineteen-year-old student at Harvard when a Connecticut regiment marched to Boston just two weeks after the battles at Lexington and Concord. He became an adjutant in the regiment and was appointed second aide-de-camp to Washington. Trumbull used his artistic abilities as a cartographer of military deployments. But his heart was in painting, and he contrived to get to France and then England in 1778 to study painting with the American artist Benjamin West.

Trumbull's ambition was to write "*in my language,* the history of our country" and particularly of "the principal events . . . of the late war." By 1785, "writing" on canvas, he had painted the Battle of Bunker Hill, acclaimed by West as "the *best picture* of a modern battle that has been painted." Trumbull went on to provide a visual documentary record of the American Revolution. Among the paintings that followed in the 1780s were ones depicting the signing of the Declaration of Independence, the death of General Hugh Mercer at the Battle of Princeton, and the climactic battle at Yorktown. Painting portraits of revolutionary leaders occupied him in the 1790s. In 1817, at the end of his career, Congress commissioned him to paint four Revolutionary War tableaux for the rotunda of the Capitol, the first commission from the federal government to an American painter.

In painting The Battle of Bunker Hill *while living in London after the Revolution, John Trumbull worked from memory; he had witnessed the battle through a spy glass. His mentor in London, Benjamin West, claimed "no man living can paint such another picture of that scene."*

Yorktown Battlefield, Colonial National Historic Park

Yorktown, Va.

Overseas Allies

Reuben Law Reed, an artistically untrained granite worker and house painter, created this rendition of George Washington and the Marquis de Lafayette at the decisive battle at Yorktown in 1781. Painted in the background are men marching to battle and aerial bombs bursting.

T he Marquis de Lafayette's emotions ran wild on the afternoon of September 15, 1781, when General George Washington rode into Williamsburg in the van of the Continental Army that he had led south in a three-week march from New York. Dashing up to Washington, Lafayette threw his arms around him "with an ardor not easily described," as Virginia's Colonel St. George Tucker wrote in his diary. For the entire summer, Lafayette had played cat and mouse with Lord General Charles Cornwallis's superior British army, trying to keep intact the several thousand Americans under his command. Always at a disadvantage, he now knew the odds had changed dramatically.

After the French fleet under Admiral François de Grasse had defeated a British flotilla just a week before in the Battle of the Chesapeake Capes, the British army was left to face the fact that its escape route was severed by the retreat of the badly mauled British ships. With a noose tightening around Cornwallis's army, six years of

Yorktown Battlefield, Colonial National Historic Park

Yorktown, VA 23690
757-898-2410
www.nps.gov/colo

NRIS 66000839
NPS

SIGNIFICANCE
The victory of the Americans and their French allies on the Yorktown Battlefield over Britain's main fighting forces ended the American Revolution. Overseas allies, particularly the Marquis de Lafayette and the French navy, played a determining role.

war were coming to an end. And the end would come on the sandy soil on the south side of the York River, which emptied into the Chesapeake Bay. There, on what would become known as the Yorktown Battlefield, the British had built earthen fortifications and artillery emplacements, preparing to make a last-ditch stand.

The Yorktown Battlefield was the dramatic site of a nine-day siege that culminated with the British surrender of about 8,300 soldiers on October 19. Here Cornwallis's army, including German auxiliary troops, had constructed a series of enclosed forts, called *redoubts*, around the small farming village of Yorktown. Within these fortifications, they positioned artillery batteries and dug a series of connected trenches. But working by night, American soldiers dug trenches outside the British lines, preparing to besiege them. By October 6 their trenches were close enough to place artillery to rain down cannon balls on the British. Doctor James Thacher, a participant at the battle described how

> the bombshells from the besiegers and the besieged are incessantly crossing each others' paths in the air. . . . In the night they appear like a fiery meteor with a blazing trail, most beautifully brilliant, ascending majestically from the mortar to a certain altitude and gradually descending to the spot where they are destined to execute their work of destruction.

Many of the batteries were French, and the bombardment pummeled the British into submission day after day. "I confess," remembered Private Joseph Martin, a soldier in the trenches, "when I saw the 'star-spangled banner' waving majestically in the very face of our implacable adversaries; it appeared like an omen of success to our enterprise."

After incessant bombardment of the British lines and the small town of Yorktown, French and American contingents conducted several attacks on the British, which led many of the British and Hessian soldiers to defect to the Americans. Finally, facing starvation and mounting casualties, Cornwallis raised the white flag. On October 19, his army marched out of Yorktown between two lines of enemy soldiers, French on one side and Americans on the other. The French band played lively music and the French regiments flew silk flags with three silver lilies. In solemn lockstep, the British

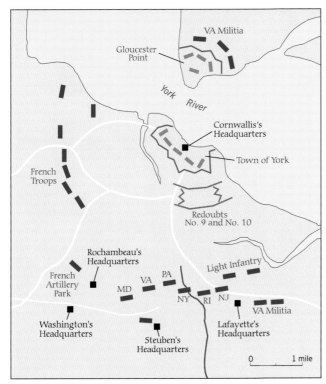

troops marched to the dirgelike tune, "The World Turned Upside Down," played by fifes and muffled drums. Lafayette ordered the American band to play "Yankee Doodle Dandy," as if to mock the British. Just ten days later, with unaccustomed speed, the Continental Congress in Philadelphia called for a Yorktown Monument to the Alliance with the French and Victory.

Most American history textbooks understate the importance of the colonies' overseas allies to the success at Yorktown. Without the French fleet driving British warships from the American coast and without 8,800 French troops and 15,000 sailors joining about 11,000 Americans, the victory would have been impossible. Near the center of the French alliance was the young, dashing Marquis de Lafayette. Almost a surrogate son to the childless Washington, Lafayette became the most important and revered European to enlist in the American cause. No other overseas ally has had so many towns, schools, hotels, streets, squares, and restaurants named after him, including one of the nation's oldest colleges, Lafayette College in Easton, Pennsylvania. When American sailors landed in France in the latter stages of World War I, they declared the debt repaid: "Lafayette, we are here."

George Washington appears in the center of this illustration of military uniforms of the Revolution. He is surrounded by Hessian, British, and French soldiers dressed for battle.

Lafayette personified what Americans said their revolution was about: selflessness, virtue, love of liberty, egalitarianism, and courage. Without the talent of foreign allies such as Lafayette and Louis Lebeque Duportail, Washington's chief engineer, the American commander in chief's precarious, resource-starved position would have been even more difficult. Many historians believe that without the support of a huge French army and navy, the colonies would have lost the war, and without financial transfusions from the French and Dutch that came when the Americans were near collapse, the British might have forced their enemy to their knees.

A wealthy aristocrat from one of France's great families, Lafayette was only nineteen in December 1776, when he met in Paris with Silas Deane, the Continental Congress's first emissary sent abroad. By this time, Deane had already sent seventeen French officers across the Atlantic. Dozens of others would follow. Lafayette eagerly put himself forward, to be given the rank of major general and to serve, as he insisted, without pay. "The moment I heard of America," Lafayette later wrote, "I loved her; the moment I knew she was fighting for freedom, I burned with a desire of bleeding for her." Expressive, romantic, impulsive, and charming, Lafayette was not a bit like the stolid, self-contained, austere Washington. But they liked—even loved—each other immensely, the twenty-five-year difference in their ages providing no obstacle to their mutual admiration and respect.

Soon after arriving in Charleston, South Carolina, Lafayette joined Washington, who immediately took a great interest in the young man. From that point, Lafayette was often at Washington's side: at the Battle of Brandywine, outside Philadelphia in September 1777; at the subsequent long, difficult winter encampment at Valley Forge; at the Battle of Monmouth in June 1778 (where the two slept side by side under a tree after the battle); and most dramatically at the Battle of Yorktown in October 1781.

The support from England's enemies in Europe—France, Holland, and Spain—turned out to be a mixed

The Colonial Gazette *printed a supplement to its October 1781 issue to spread the word of the British capitulation at Yorktown. Distributed as a broadside, it drew attention to how the French forces, at sea and on land, provided the Americans with a decisive advantage over the British.*

THE COLONIAL GAZETTE.

Num. 39.] SUPPLEMENT. Price 2 Pence

Oct. 1781

Letter from GEN. WASHINGTON to the GOVERNOR OF MARYLAND, announcing the Surrender of Cornwallis.

Camp near York, Oct., 1781.

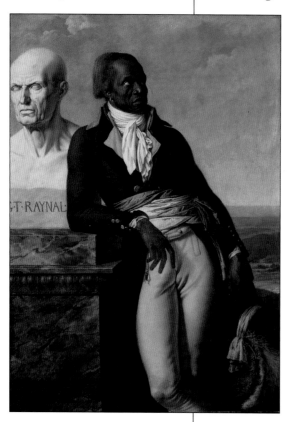

Jean-Baptiste Mars Belley, painted in 1797 by Anne Louis Girodet de Roucy-Trioson, was one of many free blacks recruited in Saint Domingue to fight against the British occupying Savannah in 1779. Belley played an important role in the Haitian Revolution that began twelve years later.

blessing. Many French and German officers wanted American commands so they could lead soldiers into battle, but they found that the young American boys were not always willing to follow them. Linguistic and cultural differences often stood between the foreign commanders and their troops. Not only that, but American officers were less than eager to be outranked by foreigners, even if they were appointed by Congress.

The alliance with France signed in the spring of 1778—the principal goal of American diplomacy for two years—was often a bitter disappointment. The admirals of the French fleet, always fearing defeat at the hands of a superior British navy, refused to commit their ships. On the other hand, the French also scorned Washington's reluctance to throw his forces directly at the British and Hessians, and wondered at the inability of the American Congress to get state commitments in men and money to pursue the war. "I swear to you," fumed Comte de Vergennes, the French minister in Philadelphia, "I have only faint confidence in the energy of the United States." Lafayette did his best to overcome this disgust; in fact, he reminded Vergennes in January 1781 that the thousands of French soldiers and dozens of warships sent to aid the colonies had mattered very little up to that point. Indeed, for the most part the French had avoided engaging the British navy off the American coast in battle and had idled in their encampments, leaving the Americans to fend for themselves—which they had done very well thus far.

Lafayette finally prevailed in 1781. He convinced the French to "give us both by vessels sent from France and by a great movement in the fleet in the islands [the West Indies], a decided naval superiority for the next campaign." Vergennes's order to bring additional French troops into the fray and his command to bring Admiral de Grasse's West Indies fleet to the Chesapeake were decisive. Combined with Washington's forces, the French commitment led to the siege of the British forces at Yorktown in October 1781, with Washington and Lafayette each commanding an element of the army. The number of French involved at Yorktown far exceeded the number of Americans, and overall, in the entire course of the war, the French commitment of 12,000 soldiers and the involvement in one way or the other of 32,000 sailors played a crucial role.

Hardly noticed in the numerous books on the American Revolution is the story of how an African-American spy moved back and forth through the Yorktown Battlefield area in order to play an important role in the British surrender at Yorktown. In March 1781, eager to play a part in repulsing the British army that had punished the South for two years, the slave of Virginia's William Armistead asked permission to enlist under Lafayette. His master agreed. That began the slave's epic service as an American spy.

Posing as a runaway slave, he crossed the British lines at Yorktown, where 8,000 British troops were bottled up by the autumn of 1781. Pretending to serve the British, as many Virginia slaves fleeing bondage since 1775 were doing, James Armistead, as he called himself, slipped away and brought to the American encampment a detailed account of the British positions. In no small way, he was responsible for the American-French victory that ended the war with Cornwallis's surrender. Lafayette met his spy in Richmond after the war and gave Armistead a testimonial: "His intelligence from the enemy's camp were industriously collected and more faithfully delivered. He perfectly acquitted himself with some important commissions I gave him and appears to me entitled to every reward his situation can admit of." In 1786, Virginia's General Assembly emancipated him for his service. Thereafter Armistead called himself James Armistead Lafayette.

The Marquis de Lafayette would forever be honored for the special role he had played in leading overseas friends to aid the American colonies in their pursuit of independence. Some of his compatriots lost their lives on American soil. Many others would remain in the United States after the war. A few became national leaders: for instance, Pierre L'Enfant, a gifted engineer and architect who had served on Baron Friedrich von Steuben's staff, remained in the United States and became the main designer of the nation's new Capitol in Washington. (Von Steuben, an experienced Prussian officer recommended

continued on page 138

Lafayette's Triumphal Return

When Lafayette returned to the United States in August 1824 at age 67, he was hailed as one of the last living links to the American Revolution. Of all the Europeans who helped the Americans gain their independence, he was the most celebrated of "liberty's friends." For thirteen months, he toured the fast-growing country, making a grand circle that took him through the southern states to the Mississippi River, up the Mississippi and Ohio rivers to the northern states, through New England, and down through the mid-Atlantic states.

In this much-publicized tour, he visited each of the 24 states. He saw Thomas Jefferson, then 81; he visited with John Adams, then 89; and he reminisced with James Armstead Lafayette, then about 76. He made an emotional pilgrimage to Washington's tomb at Mount Vernon. Accompanied by his son George Washington Lafayette, he toured dozens of battle sites where he had fought, and dozens of the buildings where he had strategized with American military leaders. At Yorktown, he listened to an address, published in the *Portsmouth and Norfolk Herald,* recounting how

> in the day of her [Virginia's] greatest peril, . . . when invading armies threatened to overrun the country, and all the horrors of war were pointed against our very dwellings, Washington selected you, his youthful friend, for the chief command and securely entrusted the defence of his native state to our courage and conduct.

Lafayette's tour launched a campaign to build monuments to revolutionary heroes. In Camden, South Carolina, he laid the cornerstone for a monument to Baron Johann de Kalb; in Savannah, cornerstones for monuments to General Nathanael Greene and General Count Kazimierz Pulaski; in Boston, a cornerstone for the Bunker Hill monument. Everywhere Lafayette went, people flocked to parades, feasts, pageants, dances, fireworks, testimonials, and concerts held in his honor. Everywhere, ancient veterans stepped forward to embrace Lafayette and tell stories about local revolutionary battles. Congress voted him $200,000 to repair his broken fortune and called him "the son of Washington," "defender of liberty," and "hero of two worlds." A mania for anything connected to him arose. Philadelphia's *Saturday Evening Post* newspaper reported

> We wrap our bodies in La Fayette coats during the day, and repose between La Fayette blankets at night. We have La Fayette bread, La Fayette butter, La Fayette beef, and La Fayette vegetables of every description, from the common turnip relish to the most dainty dish of celery. . . . Even the ladies distinguish their *proper* from *common* kisses under the title *La Fayette smooches.*

Lafayette's tour also produced a renewed interest in historic places. While Americans had swept west into the continent's interior, laid the foundations for an industrial revolution, transformed overgrown towns into cities of 100,000, and argued over the extension of slavery into new territories, they had given scant attention to preserving the past. Many of the most historic places of the revolutionary era had become decayed, burned up, torn down, or converted to new uses, their measure of worth figured commercially rather than historically.

Lafayette's tour reversed this erosion of public memory concerning the American

Revolution. In Philadelphia, the boisterous celebration for him at the old Pennsylvania State House redefined the place where the Declaration of Independence and the Constitution had been written and enhanced the reputation of Philadelphia as a historically sacred place. At the civic reception for Lafayette, the mayor referred to "this hallowed hall" and to the "Birthplace of Independence." Lafayette reinforced the point, remembering that "Here, sir, was planned the formation of our virtuous, brave, and revolutionary army, and the providential inspiration received that gave the command to our beloved matchless Washington." Within a year, the old State House was referred to as Independence Hall and the State House Yard was redesignated Independence Square. Nearly sold for private use only a decade before, Independence Hall was now on its way to becoming a national shrine, with Lafayette's invaluable assistance.

This printed linen handkerchief, produced as a souvenir for Lafayette's triumphal return to Philadelphia in 1824, shows a massive stage-prop ceremonial arch, based on the Septimus Severus Arch in Rome. Six white horses draw Lafayette through the arch in a decked-out horse-drawn carriage called a barouche.

continued from page 135

by Benjamin Franklin, had joined Washington at Valley Forge as inspector general, and had taken over the training of Continental Army troops.) Pierre Étienne du Ponceau, another member of von Steuben's staff, took up residence in Philadelphia where he became one of the city's leading intellectuals.

Lafayette's influence lasted long after the end of the war, and sometimes it involved drawing a line between himself and the man he so much revered. The most important issue that came to divide Lafayette and Washington was slavery. Looking back on the war, Lafayette claimed, "I would never have drawn my sword in the cause of America if I could have conceived that thereby I was founding a land of slavery."

Just as peace was being concluded, in February 1783, Lafayette made a startling proposal to Washington: that they purchase a plantation where they would employ emancipated slaves as tenants and in this way demonstrate how slavery could be abolished. Lafayette promised that if this succeeded in the United States, he would devote himself to "render the method

In cartoons of this kind, the British made fun of French uniforms and hairdos, but they were not laughing after the French troops and naval forces proved decisive in the victory at Yorktown.

COUNT DE ROCHAMBEAU
French General of the Land Forces in America Reviewing the French Troops

fashionable in the West Indies." Washington sounded interested in the proposal, but after he and Lafayette spent eleven days together at Mount Vernon in 1784, he declined to pursue the matter. Lafayette maintained that "if it be a wild scheme, I had rather be mad that way than to be thought wise on the other tack." But Washington begged off, pleading that he favored abolishing slavery in principle, but "to set them [the slaves] afloat at once would, I really believe, be productive of much inconvenience & mischief." Nonetheless, Lafayette remained involved in the antislavery cause. He purchased a large plantation in the French West Indian island of Cayennes and freed the slaves there, he helped found the first French society for ending the slave trade, and he became a part of the transatlantic effort to put an end to slavery.

The Yorktown Battlefield, where Lafayette made one of his most important contributions to the success of the American Revolution, has gone through several stages of life. It took a century to erect a monument of any kind to the climactic victory and more than another half-century to make a national shrine of it. The U.S. Senate Committee on Military Affairs, secured Congressional approval in 1880, arguing that "the surrender at Yorktown was the crowning success of the revolution, and its event should be commemorated by national authority." The cornerstone of the monument was laid in October 1881.

Congress began taking an interest in connecting Jamestown, Williamsburg, and Yorktown in 1902, but not until 1930 did it authorize the establishment of a Colonial National Monument for this purpose. Through the purchase of land and the development of the Colonial National Historical Park, the National Park Service brought together two centuries of early American history. Today, the park comprises more than 9,000 acres along a 23-mile scenic parkway that links the Yorktown Battlefield to Jamestown, where the first English settlement on the banks of the James River has been reconstructed.

FORT PULASKI NATIONAL MONUMENT

Monterey Square
Savannah, GA 31410
912-786-5787
www.nps.gov/fopu
NHL/NPS

The Pulaski Monument in Savannah, Georgia, commemorates a noteworthy overseas contributor to American independence: General Count Kazimierz Pulaski, the Polish patriot who gave his life in 1779 at the Battle of Savannah. In October 1779 Washington ordered an attempt to retake Savannah, which had been captured by the British in late 1778, by land and sea. He put the operation mostly in the hands of overseas friends—a remarkable combination of Polish and French officers; French troops and sailors; a regiment of free black soldiers from Santo Domingo, one of France's West Indian island colonies; and an American cavalry brigade led by Pulaski.

The Polish nobleman had fought for Polish independence against the Russians in 1772 and had fled to Paris to join a colony of refugee Poles. There he met Benjamin Franklin, who channeled him into the stream of international volunteers smitten with the idea of helping the American independence movement based on ideas of equality and liberty. Once in the American colonies, he gained command of four regiments of mounted dragoons and earned the rank of brigadier general. Pulaski fought with the Americans at Trenton and in New York; but he was killed at Savannah, where he led a cavalry assault against the British fortification.

In 1825, during his tour of the United States, the Marquis de Lafayette laid the cornerstone for a monument to Pulaski, but it took another twenty-seven years to raise the money to begin constructing the monument. Carved from Italian marble and rising fifty-five feet in Monterey Square, it was unveiled in 1856. One side of the monument displays a bas-relief of Pulaski on his horse. The shaft of the monu-ment is surmounted by a statue of Liberty. With money raised by the American Council for Polish Culture, the Polish Legion of American Veterans, and the Polish-American Congress, restoration of the monument began in 1995.

CAMDEN BATTLEFIELD

State Route 58
Camden, SC 27921
NHL

Lying six miles north of the small inland town of Camden, South Carolina, is the Camden Battlefield, its lightly timbered landscape with marshlands near two streams that have changed little in two centuries. Here, Bavarian General Johann DeKalb, an Austrian who crossed the Atlantic with Lafayette in 1777, died in battle on behalf of the American colonies. Fighting occurred here because the British had seized strategically located Camden, a Native American trading center standing at the head of the navigable Wateree River. Trying to recapture Camden, General Horatio Gates commanded the American troops, while General DeKalb commanded the Delaware and Maryland Continental soldiers. As British general Lord Charles Cornwallis overpowered the Americans on the moonless night of August 15 to 16, 1780, the fifty-nine-year-old DeKalb, a professional soldier, refused to retreat and died on the battlefield.

About 2,000 acres of the Camden Battlefield was first preserved by the Hobkirk Hill chapter of the Daughters of the American Revolution. It was designated a National Historic Landmark in 1961. DeKalb's grave is in front of the Bethesda Presbyterian Church on DeKalb Street in Camden, and a cornerstone for his monument was laid by the Marquis de Lafayette during his 1824–25 American tour. In 2000, the Palmetto Conservation Foundation and the Katawba Valley Land Trust negotiated an agreement with the Bowater Timber Company to preserve 290 acres of the battleground for use as an historic landscape. Archaeological research will be conducted in order to develop an interpretive plan of the battle.

ROCHAMBEAU HEADQUARTERS (THE ODELL HOUSE)

425 Ridge Road
Hartsdale, NY 10530
NHL

The Odell House was much smaller when it served as the 1781 headquarters of the Count de Rochambeau, whose French troops were indispensable to the ultimate American victory.

As was often the case, this unpretentious eighteenth-century farmhouse became a military nerve center of a revolutionary campaign. The Odell House had two rooms and an attic for grain storage and was built in 1732 as a tenant farmstead of the Philipsburg Manor, a vast 92,000-acre tract in the Hudson River Valley north of New York City. The shingled, framed farmhouse in Hartsdale became the headquarters of Count de Rochambeau, the general in charge of the French troops who arrived at Newport, Rhode Island, in July 1780. George Washington hoped that these troops, supported by the powerful French fleet, would save the faltering American cause.

On the tenant farm of Gilbert Bates, Rochambeau encamped his expeditionary force in the summer of 1781; and in this simple farmhouse Washington and Rochambeau sealed the French-American alliance by putting into effect the "southern plan"—an attack on the main British army under Lord Charles Cornwallis's command in Virginia. On August 18, 1781, the combined armies of Washington and Rochambeau began the long march south.

The name of Gilbert Bates, the farmer whose fields were trampled by the large French army, has never been associated with the house he occupied at the time of this crucial upturn in American affairs. Instead the house became known as the Odell House because a local revolutionary hero, Colonel John Odell, purchased the property in 1785. Ironically, this name memorializes a local war hero who later owned the house rather than its actual occupant at the time it made history. Bates had added an east wing to the original structure in 1765, and Odell added a two-story west wing after purchasing the house. Odell's heirs rebuilt and extended the house in the 1850s and again about 1900.

It was not until 1965 that Elizabeth Odell, a descendant of John Odell, deeded the house to the New York chapter of the Sons of the American Revolution. In the 1970s the new owners made extensive restorations, carefully preserving the random-width red pine flooring, walls plastered directly over the original wattle and daub, eighteenth-century doors and mantels, and original Dutch-style strap hinge hardware.

Chronology

1765

English Parliament passes Stamp Act

Riots in many towns lead to debate about "taxation without representation"

Stamp Act Congress meets in New York

Sons of Liberty formed in New York City and thereafter in many towns

1766

Declaratory Act asserts Parliament's sovereignty over the colonies after repealing Stamp Act

1767

Townshend Revenue Acts impose duties on tea, glass, paper, paints, and other items

1768

British troops sent to Boston, leading to Boston Massacre two years later

1771

Battle of Alamance pits frontier North Carolina Regulators against eastern militia led by royal governor

1772

Committee of Correspondence formed in Boston and thereafter in other cities

Angry colonists burn British schooner *Gaspee* off Rhode Island

1773

After Parliament passes Tea Act giving East India Company right to sell directly to Americans, Bostonians dump shiploads of tea into Boston harbor

1774

Coercive Acts close port of Boston, restrict provincial and town governments in Massachusetts and send additional troops to Boston

Quebec Act attaches trans-Appalachian interior north of Ohio River to government of Quebec

First Continental Congress meets in Philadelphia and forms Continental Association to boycott British imports

1775

Battles at Lexington and Concord cause 95 American and 273 British casualties

Pennsylvania Abolition Society meets in Philadelphia

Americans take Fort Ticonderoga

Second Continental Congress meets, assumes many powers of an independent government, and appoints George

Washington commander in chief of Continental Army

King George III proclaims Americans in open rebellion

Battle of Bunker Hill

Dunmore's Proclamation in Virginia promises freedom to slaves and indentured servants fleeing to the British ranks

Iroquois Confederacy pledges neutrality

1776

Thomas Paine publishes *Common Sense*

British evacuate Boston

Abigail Adams urges her husband to have political leaders consider enlarging the rights of women

William Franklin, royal governor of New Jersey, is arrested for opposing American independence

Second Continental Congress writes and passes Declaration of Independence

Eight states draft constitutions

Cherokee conduct raids on southern frontier and Americans retaliate

Small American fleet defeated by British naval forces at Valcour Bay, but Americans slow down the British invasion of northern New York

The "Webfoot Regiment" from Marblehead, Mass., helps Washington cross the Delaware River and attack the British at Trenton

1777

Most Iroquois nations join British

British occupy Philadelphia in September and decamp in June 1778

Americans victorious at Saratoga

Washington's army winters at Valley Forge

1778

The French sign treaty of alliance and commerce with the United States

John Paul Jones conducts raids on British coast

George Rogers Clark captures Kaskasia and Vincennes

Savannah falls to the British and the war shifts to the south

1779

John Sullivan destroys Iroquois villages in New York

Massachusetts state constitutional convention meets

Kazimierz Pulaski dies at the Battle of Savannah in an attempt to recapture the city from the British

1780

Pennsylvania begins gradual abolition of slavery

Charleston falls to the British

Massachusetts state constitution is ratified

Benedict Arnold deserts to the British and is burned in effigy in Philadelphia

Women in Philadelphia raise $300,000 to clothe soldiers

1781

Daniel Morgan's troops defeat British at Cowpens, S.C.

Articles of Confederation ratified by the states

John Barry fights the last battles at sea against the British

French fleet under Comte de Grasse arrives in Chesapeake Bay to help Americans siege the British at Yorktown

Cornwallis surrenders at Yorktown, ending the war

1782

New York cedes western land claims, thus beginning the creation of the Northwest Territory

1783

Peace treaty with England is signed in Paris

King's Commission on American Loyalists begins work

Massachusetts Supreme Court abolishes slavery

Further Reading

General Sources on the American Revolution

Countryman, Edward. *The American Revolution.* New York: Hill and Wang, 1985.

Nash, Gary B. *The Urban Crucible: The Northern Seaports and the Origins of the American Revolution.* Cambridge, Mass.: Harvard University Press, 1986.

Rhoden, Nancy L. and Ian K. Steele, eds. *The Human Tradition in the American Revolution.* Wilmington, Del.: Scholarly Resources, 2000.

Smith, Page. *A New Age Now Begins: A People's History of the American Revolution.* 2 vols. New York: Penguin, 1976.

Lexington Green

Bernon Tourtellot, Arthur. *Lexington and Concord: The Beginning of the War of the American Revolution.* New York: W.W. Norton, 1963.

Fischer, David Hackett. *Paul Revere's Ride.* New York: Oxford University Press, 1994.

———. *Concord: The Social History of a New England Town, 1750–1850.* Waltham, Mass.: np, 1983.

Maier, Pauline. *The Old Revolutionaries: Political Lives in the Age of Samuel Adams.* New York: Norton, 1980.

Malcolm, Joyce Lee. *The Scene of the Battle, 1775, Historic Grounds Report: Minute Man National Historic Park.* Boston: National Park Service, 1985.

Young, Alfred F. *The Shoemaker and the Tea Party: Memory and the American Revolution.* Boston: Beacon Press, 1999.

Independence Hall

Foner, Eric. *Tom Paine and Revolutionary America.* New York: Oxford University Press, 1976.

Greiff, Constance M. *Independence: The Creation of a National Park.* Philadelphia: University of Pennsylvania Press, 1987.

Maier, Pauline. *American Scripture: Making the Declaration of Independence.* New York: Knopf, 1997.

Mires, Charlene. *Independence Hall in American Memory.* Philadelphia: University of Pennsylvania Press, 2002.

Riley, Edward M. *The Story of Independence Hall.* Harpers Ferry, W.Va.: National Park Service, 1954.

Valley Forge National Historic Park

Bodle, Wayne. *Valley Forge Winter.* State College: Pennsylvania State University Press, 2003.

Hoyt, Bill Alfred. *Valley Forge: The Making of an Army.* New York: Harper, 1952.

Martin, James Kirby, ed. *Ordinary Courage: The Revolutionary War Adventures of Joseph Plumb Martin.* St. James, N.Y.: Brandywine, 1993.

Mayer, Holly A. *Belonging to the Army: Camp Followers and Community during the American Revolution.* Columbia: University of South Carolina Press, 1996.

Menz, Katherine. *Washington's Headquarters, Valley Forge National Historical Park.* Harpers Ferry, W.Va.: National Park Service, 1990.

Pollarine, Barbara. *Great and Capital Changes: An Account of the Valley Forge Encampment.* Gettysburg, Md.: Thomas, 1993.

Royster, Charles. *A Revolutionary People in Arms: The Continental Army and American Character,*

1775–1783. Chapel Hill: University of North Carolina Press, 1979.

Shy, John. *A People Numerous and Armed: Reflections on the Military Struggle for American Independence.* New York: Oxford University Press, 1976.

Treese, Lorett. *Valley Forge: Making and Remaking a National Symbol.* University Park: Pennsylvania State Univ. Press, 1995.

Marblehead Historic District

Chamberlain, Samuel. *Old Marblehead: A Camera Impression.* New York: Hastings House, 1975.

Billias, George A. *John Glover and His Marblehead Mariners.* New York: Holt, 1960.

Hercher, Gail P. *Victorian Marblehead.* Marblehead, Mass.: Sometime Press, 1980.

Lord, Priscilla and Virginia Ganage. *Marblehead: The Spirit of '76 Lives Here.* Philadelphia: Chilton, 1972.

Morison, Samuel Eliot. *John Paul Jones: A Sailor's Biography.* Boston: Little, Brown, 1959.

Faneuil Hall

Beach, Stewart. *Samuel Adams, the Fateful Years, 1764–1776.* New York: Dodd, Mead, 1965.

Hawke, David Freeman. *Benjamin Rush: Revolutionary Gadfly.* Indianapolis: Bobbs Merrill, 1971.

Mayer, Henry. *A Son of Thunder: Patrick Henry and the American Republic.* New York: Watts, 1986.

Monkhouse, Christopher P. *Faneuil Hall Market: An Account of Its Many Likenesses.* Boston: Bostonian Society, 1969.

Wilson, Susan. *Boston Sites and Insights: A Multicultural Guide to Fifty Historic Landmarks in and around Boston.* Boston: Beacon Press, 1994.

Wood, Gordon S. *Radicalism and the American Revolution.* New York: Knopf, 1992.

Peyton Randolph House

Whiffen, Marcus. *The Eighteenth-Century Houses of Williamsburg: A Study in Architecture and Building.* Williamsburg, Va.: Colonial Williamsburg, 1984.

Chamberlain, Samuel. *Behold Williamsburg: A Pictorial Tour of Virginia's Colonial Capital.* New York: Hastings House, 1947.

Handler, Richard and Eric Gable. *The New History in an Old Museum: Creating the Past at Colonial Williamsburg.* Durham, N.C.: Duke University Press, 1997.

Kaplan, Sidney and Emma Nogrady Kaplan. *The Black Presence in the Era of the American Revolution.* Amherst: University of Massachusetts Press, 1989.

Nash, Gary B. *Race and Revolution.* Madison, Wis : Madison House, 1990.

Quarles, Benjamin. *The Negro in the American Revolution.* Chapel Hill: University of North Carolina Press, 1996.

Winch, Julie. *A Gentleman of Color: The Life of James Forten.* New York: Oxford University Press, 2002.

John and Abigail Adams House

Gundersen, Joan. *To Be Useful to the World: Women in Revolutionary America, 1740–1790.* Englewood Cliffs, N.J.: Prentice Hall, 1996.

Harris, Wilhelmina S. *Adams National Historic Site: A Family's Legacy in America.* Harpers Ferry, W.Va.: National Park Service, 1983.

Kerber, Linda. *Women of the Republic: Intellect and Ideology in Revolutionary America.* Chapel Hill: University of North Carolina Press, 1980.

Withey, Lynne. *Dearest Friend: A Life of Abigail Adams.* New York: Free Press, 1981.

Johnson Hall

Calloway, Colin. *The American Revolution in Indian Country: Crisis and Diversity in Native American Communities.* Cambridge, England: Cambridge University Press, 1995.

Hamilton, Milton W. *Sir William Johnson: Colonial American, 1715–1763.* Port Washington, N.Y.: National University, 1976.

Thompson Kelsay, Isabel. *Joseph Brant, 1743–1807.* Syracuse, N.Y.: Syracuse University Press, 1984.

Old Saint Mary's Episcopal Church

Burr, Nelson R. *The Anglican Church in New Jersey.* Philadelphia: Church Historical Society, 1954.

Nelson, William H. *The American Tory.* Boston: Beacon Press, 1961.

Randall, Willard Sterne. *A Little Revenge: Benjamin Franklin and His Son.* Boston: Little, Brown, 1984.

Old South Meeting House

Akers, Charles W. *The Divine Politician: Samuel Cooper and the American Revolution in Boston.* Boston: Northeastern University Press, 1982.

Bloch, Ruth. *Visionary Republic: Millennial Themes in American Thought, 1756–1800.* New York: Cambridge University Press, 1985.

Burdett, Everett W. *History of the Old South Meeting-house in Boston.* Boston: B.B. Russell, 1877.

Dunwell, Steve and Blanche M. G. Linden. *Boston Freedom Trail.* Boston: Back Bay Press, 1996.

Wilson, Susan. *Boston Sites and Insights: A Multicultural Guide to Fifty Historic Landmarks in and around Boston.* Boston: Beacon Press, 1994.

Francis Hopkinson House

Di Ionno, Mark. *A Guide to New Jersey's Revolutionary War Trail for Families and History Buffs.* New Brunswick, N.J.: Rutgers University Press, 2000.

Sellers, Charles Coleman. *Charles Willson Peale.* New York: Scribner, 1969.

Silverman, Kenneth. *A Cultural History of the American Revolution.* New York: Crowell, 1976.

Society of Colonial Wars in the State of New Jersey. *The Historic Roadsides of New Jersey.* Trenton, N.J.: Innes & Sons, 1928.

Yorktown Battlefield

Davis, Burke. *The Campaign that Won America.* New York: Dial Press, 1970.

Kramer, Lloyd S. *Lafayette in Two Worlds: Public Cultures and Personal Identities in an Age of Revolutions.* Chapel Hill: University of North Carolina Press, 1996.

Symonds, Craig L. *A Battlefield Atlas of the American Revolution.* Annapolis, Md.: Nautical and Aviation Publishing Co., 1986.

Szymanski, Leszek. *Casimir Pulaski: A Hero of the American Revolution.* New York: Hippocene, 1994.

Index

The National Register of Historic Places, National Park Service

The National Register of Historic Places is the official U.S. list of historic places worthy of preservation. Authorized under the National Historic Preservation Act of 1966, the National Register is part of a national program to coordinate and support public and private efforts to identify, evaluate, and protect America's historic and archeological resources. The National Register is administered by the National Park Service, which is part of the U.S. Department of the Interior.

Properties listed in the National Register include districts, sites, buildings, structures, and objects that are significant in U.S. history, architecture, archaeology, engineering, and culture. Places range from ancient Indian pueblos, to homes of writers or philanthropists, to bridges, to commercial districts. Among the tens of thousands of listings are: all historic areas in the National Park System; National Historic Landmarks; and properties nominated for their significance to communities, states, or the nation. The public can find information about these places on the web from the National Register Information System (NRIS) or request copies of documentation files.

For more information about the National Register of Historic Places, visit our Web site at www.cr.nps.gov/nr; phone 202-354-2213; fax 202-371-2229; e-mail nr_info@nps.gov; or write National Register of Historic Places, National Park Service, 1849 C Street, NW, Washington, DC 20240.

Teaching with Historic Places

The Teaching with Historic Places program (TwHP) uses places listed in the National Register to enrich and enliven the study of history, social studies, geography and other subjects. Historic places have the power to make us more aware of our connection to the people and events that preceded us. It is possible to experience that "sense of place" whether or not site visits are possible. By actively investigating places and documentation about them, students can develop enthusiasm and curiosity while they enjoy a historian's sense of discovery and learn critical skills.

A series of lessons based on places around the country forms the cornerstone of the TwHP program. It includes Revolutionary and Civil War battlefields, presidential homes, churches that hosted Civil Rights meetings, places where women made history, and much more. Each lesson plan includes an activity that leads students to research the history and historic places in their own communities. TwHP lessons are free and available online, where they are indexed by state, historic theme, time period, and the National Standards for History.

For more information about the award-winning TwHP program or to acquire the lesson plans, visit the TwHP Web site at www.cr.nps.gov/nr/twhp; phone 202-354-2213; fax 202-371-2229; e-mail nr_twhp@nps.gov; or write Teaching with Historic Places, National Register of Historic Places, National Park Service, 1849 C Street, NW, Washington, DC 20240.

Acknowledgments

Jim Horton, editor of the American Landmarks series, has been a stalwart and inspiring colleague in shepherding this book through various stages. Nancy Toff, vice president and editorial director of the Young Adult Reference division of Oxford University Press, has done equally commendable service, keeping the author faithful to the overall design of the series and offering useful suggestions and criticisms of several drafts. Beth M. Boland, historian at the National Register of Historic Places and program manager of Teaching with Historic Places was invaluable in suggesting particular historic sites and in reading an early draft of the manuscript with care. I am indebted also to Carol D. Shull, Keeper of the National Register of Historic Places and Chief of the National Historic Landmarks Survey, for facilitating access to the records and histories of various sites that appear in this book. Nancy Hirsch at Oxford University Press used a fine-toothed comb to eliminate errors in the manuscript and bring maximum clarity to it. At UCLA, Samantha Gervase Holtkamp and Grace Lu provided able research assistance.

Gilder Lehrman Institute of American History

The Gilder Lehrman Institute of American History promotes the study and love of American history. It organizes seminars and enrichment programs for teachers and National Park Service educators; creates history-centered high schools nationwide; supports and produces publications and traveling exhibitions for students and the general public; sponsors lectures by historians; develops electronic media projects, including the Institute's website; establishes research centers at universities and libraries; and grants and oversees fellowships for scholars to work in the Gilder Lehrman Collection and in other archives of American history. The Gilder Lehrman Institute may be contacted at:

19 W. 44th Street, Suite 500
New York, NY 10036-5902
646-366-9666
fax 646-366-9669
http://www.gilderlehrman.org

Oxford University Press would especially like to thank the Gilder Lehrman Institute of American History for the following images: Gilder Lehrman Collection, courtesy of Gilder Lehrman Institute of American History, New York: 2, 19, 20, 52, 71, 132.

Picture Credits

Albany Institute of History & Art: 7, 86, Gift of Laura Munsell Tremaine: 87; Abby Aldrich Rockefeller Folk Art Museum, Colonial Williamsburg Foundation:129; © Richard Beauchesne, 2002: 55; The Boston Public Library: 89; Bostonian Society Library and Special Collections: 59; Chicago Historical Society: 41; Christ Church: 117; Colonial Williamsburg Foundation: 66, 68; Courtesy of Conn. D.A.R.: 127; Connecticut Historical Society, Hartford, Connecticut: 7, 14; Fenimore Art Museum, Cooperstown, New York, photo Richard Walker: 76; Barbara Frake, courtesy of St. Mary's Parish: 98, 100; Courtesy of the Frick Art Reference Library: 104; © Giraudon/Art Resource NY: 134; Greater Boston CVB: 57; Courtesy of The Historical Society of Pennsylvania Collection, Atwater Kent Museum of Philadelphia: 29, 122; John Hopf: 119; Courtesy of Jeffery Howe: 49, 107; Courtesy of www.hvnet.com: 141; R. Lautman/Monticello: 36; Lexington Historical Society: 17; The Library Company of Philadelphia: 62, 73; Library of Congress: 18, 24, 26, 31, 32, 42, 43, 44, 48, 53, 67, 72, 85, 95, 112, 115, 124, 128, 133, 138, 108, 16 (bottom), 54, 80, 88; Courtesy of Philip McAuliffe: 120; ©1992 The Metropolitan Museum of Art, Gift of John Stewart Kennedy, 1897. (97.34): 69; Courtesy of The Mount Vernon Ladies' Association: 46; © 2002 Museum of Fine Arts, Boston. Bequest of Winslow Warren, 1931: 81, Deposited by the City of Boston, L-R 30.76c: 60, Gift of Joseph W. Revere, William B. Revere and Edward H. R. Revere, 1930: 21; Courtesy of National Center for the American Revolution/ The Valley Forge Historical Society: 40; Courtesy National Museum of The American Indian, Smithsonian Institution: 91; National Park Service; 16 (top), 23, Colonial National Park: 130; Collection of the New-York Historical Society negative number 1867.314: 92, negative number 48257: 78; Courtesy Paul Revere Memorial Association. Photo: Art of Light.: 22; Peabody Essex Museum: 50; Courtesy of the Pennsylvania Academy of the Fine Arts, Philadelphia. Gift of Mrs. Sarah Harrison (The Joseph Harrison, Jr. Collection): 125; Courtesy of the Historic Collections of Pennsylvania Hospital, Philadelphia: 64; The Harry T. Peters Collection, Museum of the City of New York: 3; Stahl Associates/Sam Sweezy: 7, 108, 109; The Trustees of Reservations: 96; Courtesy U.S. Naval Academy Museum: 56; U.S. Dept. of Interior, National Park Service, Adams National Historical Park: 75, 83; Courtesy of Valley Forge Historical Society: 37; Courtesy of Winterthur Museum: 34, 137

Text Credits

p. 28: L. H. Butterfield, ed., *The Adams Papers, Series II, Adams Family Correspondence, Vol. 2.* New York: Athenaeum, 1965, pp. 27–28.

p. 39: James Kirby Martin, ed., *Ordinary Courage: The Revolutionary War Adventures of Joseph Plumb Martin.* St. James, N.Y.: Brandywine, 1993, 62–63.

p. 54: Gardiner W. Allen, *A Naval History of the American Revolution.* Reprint, 2 vols. Williamstown, Mass.: Corner House, 1970, Vol. 2, pp. 634–35.

p. 70: Sidney Kaplan and Emma Nogrady Kaplan, *The Black Presence in the Era of the American Revolution.* Amherst: University of Massachusetts Press, 1989, pp. 13, 15.

p. 72: Julian D. Mason, Jr., ed., *The Poems of Phillis Wheatley.* Chapel Hill: University of North Carolina Press, 1989, p. 131, 83.

p. 78: Butterfield, L. H., Marc Friedlaender, and Mary-Jo Kline, eds., *The book of Abigail and John: Selected letters of the Adams family, 1762–1784.* Cambridge, Mass.: Harvard University Press, 1975, pp. 184-85.

p. 94: Colin G. Calloway, *First Peoples: A Documentary Survey of American Indian History.* Boston: Bedford/St. Martin's, 1999, pp. 187–88.

p. 103: Seabury, Samuel. *Free Thoughts on the Proceedings of the Continental Congress.* New York: James Rivington, 1774, pp. 15–19.

p. 113: Joseph Warren, *An Oration Delivered March Sixth 1775.* Boston, 1775, pp. 20–22. Thomas Bolton, *An Oration Delivered March Fifteenth 1775.* Boston, 1775, pp. 1–2.

p. 123: *A New Song to The Tune of Hearts of Oak.* Philadelphia, 1768. Billings, William, *The New-England Psalm-Singer.* Boston: Edes and Gill, 1770, p. 91.